Q-109

TEST YOUR KNOWLEDG

THIS IS YOUR **PASSBOOK®** FOR ...

# SMALL ENGINE REPAIR

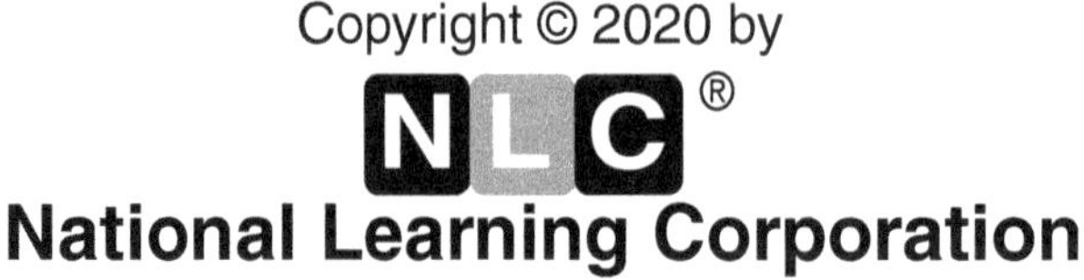



212 Michael Drive, Syosset, NY 11791
(516) 921-8888 • www.passbooks.com
E-mail: info@passbooks.com

PUBLISHED IN THE UNITED STATES OF AMERICA

# PASSBOOK® SERIES

THE *PASSBOOK® SERIES* has been created to prepare applicants and candidates for the ultimate academic battlefield – the examination room.

At some time in our lives, each and every one of us may be required to take an examination – for validation, matriculation, admission, qualification, registration, certification, or licensure.

Based on the assumption that every applicant or candidate has met the basic formal educational standards, has taken the required number of courses, and read the necessary texts, the *PASSBOOK® SERIES* furnishes the one special preparation which may assure passing with confidence, instead of failing with insecurity. Examination questions – together with answers – are furnished as the basic vehicle for study so that the mysteries of the examination and its compounding difficulties may be eliminated or diminished by a sure method.

This book is meant to help you pass your examination provided that you qualify and are serious in your objective.

The entire field is reviewed through the huge store of content information which is succinctly presented through a provocative and challenging approach – the question-and-answer method.

A climate of success is established by furnishing the correct answers at the end of each test.

You soon learn to recognize types of questions, forms of questions, and patterns of questioning. You may even begin to anticipate expected outcomes.

You perceive that many questions are repeated or adapted so that you can gain acute insights, which may enable you to score many sure points.

You learn how to confront new questions, or types of questions, and to attack them confidently and work out the correct answers.

You note objectives and emphases, and recognize pitfalls and dangers, so that you may make positive educational adjustments.

Moreover, you are kept fully informed in relation to new concepts, methods, practices, and directions in the field.

You discover that you arre actually taking the examination all the time: you are preparing for the examination by "taking" an examination, not by reading extraneous and/or supererogatory textbooks.

In short, this PASSBOOK®, used directedly, should be an important factor in helping you to pass your test.

# HOW TO TAKE A TEST

You have studied long, hard and conscientiously.

With your official admission card in hand, and your heart pounding, you have been admitted to the examination room.

You note that there are several hundred other applicants in the examination room waiting to take the same test.

They all appear to be equally well prepared.

You know that nothing but your best effort will suffice. The "moment of truth" is at hand: you now have to demonstrate objectively, in writing, your knowledge of content and your understanding of subject matter.

You are fighting the most important battle of your life—to pass and/or score high on an examination which will determine your career and provide the economic basis for your livelihood.

What extra, special things should you know and should you do in taking the examination?

## I. YOU MUST PASS AN EXAMINATION

### *A. WHAT EVERY CANDIDATE SHOULD KNOW*

Examination applicants often ask us for help in preparing for the written test. What can I study in advance? What kinds of questions will be asked? How will the test be given? How will the papers be graded?

### *B. HOW ARE EXAMS DEVELOPED?*

Examinations are carefully written by trained technicians who are specialists in the field known as "psychological measurement," in consultation with recognized authorities in the field of work that the test will cover. These experts recommend the subject matter areas or skills to be tested; only those knowledges or skills important to your success on the job are included. The most reliable books and source materials available are used as references. Together, the experts and technicians judge the difficulty level of the questions.

Test technicians know how to phrase questions so that the problem is clearly stated. Their ethics do not permit "trick" or "catch" questions. Questions may have been tried out on sample groups, or subjected to statistical analysis, to determine their usefulness.

Written tests are often used in combination with performance tests, ratings of training and experience, and oral interviews. All of these measures combine to form the best-known means of finding the right person for the right job.

## II. HOW TO PASS THE WRITTEN TEST

### *A. BASIC STEPS*

1) Study the announcement

How, then, can you know what subjects to study? Our best answer is: "Learn as much as possible about the class of positions for which you've applied." The exam will test the knowledge, skills and abilities needed to do the work.

Your most valuable source of information about the position you want is the official exam announcement. This announcement lists the training and experience qualifications. Check these standards and apply only if you come reasonably close to meeting them. Many jurisdictions preview the written test in the exam announcement by including a section called "Knowledge and Abilities Required," "Scope of the Examination," or some similar heading. Here you will find out specifically what fields will be tested.

2) Choose appropriate study materials

If the position for which you are applying is technical or advanced, you will read more advanced, specialized material. If you are already familiar with the basic principles of your field, elementary textbooks would waste your time. Concentrate on advanced textbooks and technical periodicals. Think through the concepts and review difficult problems in your field.

These are all general sources. You can get more ideas on your own initiative, following these leads. For example, training manuals and publications of the government agency which employs workers in your field can be useful, particularly for technical and professional positions. A letter or visit to the government department involved may result in more specific study suggestions, and certainly will provide you with a more definite idea of the exact nature of the position you are seeking.

3) Study this book!

## III. KINDS OF TESTS

Tests are used for purposes other than measuring knowledge and ability to perform specified duties. For some positions, it is equally important to test ability to make adjustments to new situations or to profit from training. In others, basic mental abilities not dependent on information are essential. Questions which test these things may not appear as pertinent to the duties of the position as those which test for knowledge and information. Yet they are often highly important parts of a fair examination. For very general questions, it is almost impossible to help you direct your study efforts. What we can do is to point out some of the more common of these general abilities needed in public service positions and describe some typical questions.

1) General information

Broad, general information has been found useful for predicting job success in some kinds of work. This is tested in a variety of ways, from vocabulary lists to questions about current events. Basic background in some field of work, such as sociology or economics, may be sampled in a group of questions. Often these are principles which have become familiar to most persons through exposure rather than through formal training. It is difficult to advise you how to study for these questions; being alert to the world around you is our best suggestion.

2) Verbal ability

An example of an ability needed in many positions is verbal or language ability. Verbal ability is, in brief, the ability to use and understand words. Vocabulary and grammar tests are typical measures of this ability. Reading comprehension or paragraph interpretation questions are common in many kinds of civil service tests. You are given a paragraph of written material and asked to find its central meaning.

## IV. KINDS OF QUESTIONS

### 1. Multiple-choice Questions

Most popular of the short-answer questions is the "multiple choice" or "best answer" question. It can be used, for example, to test for factual knowledge, ability to solve problems or judgment in meeting situations found at work.

A multiple-choice question is normally one of three types:

- It can begin with an incomplete statement followed by several possible endings. You are to find the one ending which *best* completes the statement, although some of the others may not be entirely wrong.
- It can also be a complete statement in the form of a question which is answered by choosing one of the statements listed.
- It can be in the form of a problem – again you select the best answer.

Here is an example of a multiple-choice question with a discussion which should give you some clues as to the method for choosing the right answer:

When an employee has a complaint about his assignment, the action which will *best* help him overcome his difficulty is to

A. discuss his difficulty with his coworkers
B. take the problem to the head of the organization
C. take the problem to the person who gave him the assignment
D. say nothing to anyone about his complaint

In answering this question, you should study each of the choices to find which is best. Consider choice "A" – Certainly an employee may discuss his complaint with fellow employees, but no change or improvement can result, and the complaint remains unresolved. Choice "B" is a poor choice since the head of the organization probably does not know what assignment you have been given, and taking your problem to him is known as "going over the head" of the supervisor. The supervisor, or person who made the assignment, is the person who can clarify it or correct any injustice. Choice "C" is, therefore, correct. To say nothing, as in choice "D," is unwise. Supervisors have and interest in knowing the problems employees are facing, and the employee is seeking a solution to his problem.

**2. True/False**

**3. Matching Questions**

Matching an answer from a column of choices within another column.

## V. RECORDING YOUR ANSWERS

Computer terminals are used more and more today for many different kinds of exams.

For an examination with very few applicants, you may be told to record your answers in the test booklet itself. Separate answer sheets are much more common. If this separate answer sheet is to be scored by machine – and this is often the case – it is highly important that you mark your answers correctly in order to get credit.

## VI. BEFORE THE TEST

YOUR PHYSICAL CONDITION IS IMPORTANT

If you are not well, you can't do your best work on tests. If you are half asleep, you can't do your best either. Here are some tips:

1) Get about the same amount of sleep you usually get. Don't stay up all night before the test, either partying or worrying—DON'T DO IT!
2) If you wear glasses, be sure to wear them when you go to take the test. This goes for hearing aids, too.
3) If you have any physical problems that may keep you from doing your best, be sure to tell the person giving the test. If you are sick or in poor health, you relay cannot do your best on any test. You can always come back and take the test some other time.

Common sense will help you find procedures to follow to get ready for an examination. Too many of us, however, overlook these sensible measures. Indeed, nervousness and fatigue have been found to be the most serious reasons why applicants fail to do their best on civil service tests. Here is a list of reminders:

- Begin your preparation early – Don't wait until the last minute to go scurrying around for books and materials or to find out what the position is all about.
- Prepare continuously – An hour a night for a week is better than an all-night cram session. This has been definitely established. What is more, a night a week for a month will return better dividends than crowding your study into a shorter period of time.
- Locate the place of the exam – You have been sent a notice telling you when and where to report for the examination. If the location is in a different town or otherwise unfamiliar to you, it would be well to inquire the best route and learn something about the building.
- Relax the night before the test – Allow your mind to rest. Do not study at all that night. Plan some mild recreation or diversion; then go to bed early and get a good night's sleep.
- Get up early enough to make a leisurely trip to the place for the test – This way unforeseen events, traffic snarls, unfamiliar buildings, etc. will not upset you.

- Dress comfortably – A written test is not a fashion show. You will be known by number and not by name, so wear something comfortable.
- Leave excess paraphernalia at home – Shopping bags and odd bundles will get in your way. You need bring only the items mentioned in the official notice you received; usually everything you need is provided. Do not bring reference books to the exam. They will only confuse those last minutes and be taken away from you when in the test room.
- Arrive somewhat ahead of time – If because of transportation schedules you must get there very early, bring a newspaper or magazine to take your mind off yourself while waiting.
- Locate the examination room – When you have found the proper room, you will be directed to the seat or part of the room where you will sit. Sometimes you are given a sheet of instructions to read while you are waiting. Do not fill out any forms until you are told to do so; just read them and be prepared.
- Relax and prepare to listen to the instructions
- If you have any physical problem that may keep you from doing your best, be sure to tell the test administrator. If you are sick or in poor health, you really cannot do your best on the exam. You can come back and take the test some other time.

## VII. AT THE TEST

The day of the test is here and you have the test booklet in your hand. The temptation to get going is very strong. Caution! There is more to success than knowing the right answers. You must know how to identify your papers and understand variations in the type of short-answer question used in this particular examination. Follow these suggestions for maximum results from your efforts:

### 1) Cooperate with the monitor

The test administrator has a duty to create a situation in which you can be as much at ease as possible. He will give instructions, tell you when to begin, check to see that you are marking your answer sheet correctly, and so on. He is not there to guard you, although he will see that your competitors do not take unfair advantage. He wants to help you do your best.

### 2) Listen to all instructions

Don't jump the gun! Wait until you understand all directions. In most civil service tests you get more time than you need to answer the questions. So don't be in a hurry. Read each word of instructions until you clearly understand the meaning. Study the examples, listen to all announcements and follow directions. Ask questions if you do not understand what to do.

### 3) Identify your papers

Civil service exams are usually identified by number only. You will be assigned a number; you must not put your name on your test papers. Be sure to copy your number correctly. Since more than one exam may be given, copy your exact examination title.

### 4) Plan your time

Unless you are told that a test is a "speed" or "rate of work" test, speed itself is usually not important. Time enough to answer all the questions will be provided, but this does not mean that you have all day. An overall time limit has been set. Divide the total time (in minutes) by the number of questions to determine the approximate time you have for each question.

**5) Do not linger over difficult questions**

If you come across a difficult question, mark it with a paper clip (useful to have along) and come back to it when you have been through the booklet. One caution if you do this – be sure to skip a number on your answer sheet as well. Check often to be sure that you have not lost your place and that you are marking in the row numbered the same as the question you are answering.

**6) Read the questions**

Be sure you know what the question asks! Many capable people are unsuccessful because they failed to *read* the questions correctly.

**7) Answer all questions**

Unless you have been instructed that a penalty will be deducted for incorrect answers, it is better to guess than to omit a question.

**8) Speed tests**

It is often better NOT to guess on speed tests. It has been found that on timed tests people are tempted to spend the last few seconds before time is called in marking answers at random – without even reading them – in the hope of picking up a few extra points. To discourage this practice, the instructions may warn you that your score will be "corrected" for guessing. That is, a penalty will be applied. The incorrect answers will be deducted from the correct ones, or some other penalty formula will be used.

**9) Review your answers**

If you finish before time is called, go back to the questions you guessed or omitted to give them further thought. Review other answers if you have time.

**10) Return your test materials**

If you are ready to leave before others have finished or time is called, take ALL your materials to the monitor and leave quietly. Never take any test material with you. The monitor can discover whose papers are not complete, and taking a test booklet may be grounds for disqualification.

## VIII. EXAMINATION TECHNIQUES

1) Read the general instructions carefully. These are usually printed on the first page of the exam booklet. As a rule, these instructions refer to the timing of the examination; the fact that you should not start work until the signal and must stop work at a signal, etc. If there are any *special* instructions, such as a choice of questions to be answered, make sure that you note this instruction carefully.

2) When you are ready to start work on the examination, that is as soon as the signal has been given, read the instructions to each question booklet, underline any key words or phrases, such as *least*, *best*, *outline*, *describe*

and the like. In this way you will tend to answer as requested rather than discover on reviewing your paper that you *listed without describing*, that you selected the *worst* choice rather than the *best* choice, etc.

3) If the examination is of the objective or multiple-choice type – that is, each question will also give a series of possible answers: A, B, C or D, and you are called upon to select the best answer and write the letter next to that answer on your answer paper – it is advisable to start answering each question in turn. There may be anywhere from 50 to 100 such questions in the three or four hours allotted and you can see how much time would be taken if you read through all the questions before beginning to answer any. Furthermore, if you come across a question or group of questions which you know would be difficult to answer, it would undoubtedly affect your handling of all the other questions.

4) If the examination is of the essay type and contains but a few questions, it is a moot point as to whether you should read all the questions before starting to answer any one. Of course, if you are given a choice – say five out of seven and the like – then it is essential to read all the questions so you can eliminate the two that are most difficult. If, however, you are asked to answer all the questions, there may be danger in trying to answer the easiest one first because you may find that you will spend too much time on it. The best technique is to answer the first question, then proceed to the second, etc.

5) Time your answers. Before the exam begins, write down the time it started, then add the time allowed for the examination and write down the time it must be completed, then divide the time available somewhat as follows:
   - If 3-1/2 hours are allowed, that would be 210 minutes. If you have 80 objective-type questions, that would be an average of 2-1/2 minutes per question. Allow yourself no more than 2 minutes per question, or a total of 160 minutes, which will permit about 50 minutes to review.
   - If for the time allotment of 210 minutes there are 7 essay questions to answer, that would average about 30 minutes a question. Give yourself only 25 minutes per question so that you have about 35 minutes to review.

6) The most important instruction is to *read each question* and make sure you know what is wanted. The second most important instruction is to *time yourself properly* so that you answer every question. The third most important instruction is to *answer every question*. Guess if you have to but include something for each question. Remember that you will receive no credit for a blank and will probably receive some credit if you write something in answer to an essay question. If you guess a letter – say "B" for a multiple-choice question – you may have guessed right. If you leave a blank as an answer to a multiple-choice question, the examiners may respect your feelings but it will not add a point to your score. Some exams may penalize you for wrong answers, so in such cases *only*, you may not want to guess unless you have some basis for your answer.

7) Suggestions

a. Objective-type questions

1. Examine the question booklet for proper sequence of pages and questions
2. Read all instructions carefully
3. Skip any question which seems too difficult; return to it after all other questions have been answered
4. Apportion your time properly; do not spend too much time on any single question or group of questions
5. Note and underline key words – *all, most, fewest, least, best, worst, same, opposite,* etc.
6. Pay particular attention to negatives
7. Note unusual option, e.g., unduly long, short, complex, different or similar in content to the body of the question
8. Observe the use of “hedging” words – *probably, may, most likely,* etc.
9. Make sure that your answer is put next to the same number as the question
10. Do not second-guess unless you have good reason to believe the second answer is definitely more correct
11. Cross out original answer if you decide another answer is more accurate; do not erase until you are ready to hand your paper in
12. Answer all questions; guess unless instructed otherwise
13. Leave time for review

b. Essay questions

1. Read each question carefully
2. Determine exactly what is wanted. Underline key words or phrases.
3. Decide on outline or paragraph answer
4. Include many different points and elements unless asked to develop any one or two points or elements
5. Show impartiality by giving pros and cons unless directed to select one side only
6. Make and write down any assumptions you find necessary to answer the questions
7. Watch your English, grammar, punctuation and choice of words
8. Time your answers; don’t crowd material

8) Answering the essay question

Most essay questions can be answered by framing the specific response around several key words or ideas. Here are a few such key words or ideas:

M’s: manpower, materials, methods, money, management

P’s: purpose, program, policy, plan, procedure, practice, problems, pitfalls, personnel, public relations

a. Six basic steps in handling problems:

1. Preliminary plan and background development
2. Collect information, data and facts
3. Analyze and interpret information, data and facts
4. Analyze and develop solutions as well as make recommendations

5. Prepare report and sell recommendations
6. Install recommendations and follow up effectiveness

b. Pitfalls to avoid

1. *Taking things for granted* – A statement of the situation does not necessarily imply that each of the elements is necessarily true; for example, a complaint may be invalid and biased so that all that can be taken for granted is that a complaint has been registered
2. *Considering only one side of a situation* – Wherever possible, indicate several alternatives and then point out the reasons you selected the best one
3. *Failing to indicate follow up* – Whenever your answer indicates action on your part, make certain that you will take proper follow-up action to see how successful your recommendations, procedures or actions turn out to be
4. *Taking too long in answering any single question* – Remember to time your answers properly

# EXAMINATION SECTION

# EXAMINATION SECTION
# TEST 1

DIRECTIONS: Each question or incomplete statement is followed by several suggested answers or completions. Select the one that BEST answers the question or completes the statement. *PRINT THE LETTER OF THE CORRECT ANSWER IN THE SPACE AT THE RIGHT.*

Questions 1-6.

DIRECTIONS: Questions 1 through 6 refer to the figure below, a side view of a basic valve assembly. Place the letter that corresponds to each diagrammed component in the space at the right next to the component's name.

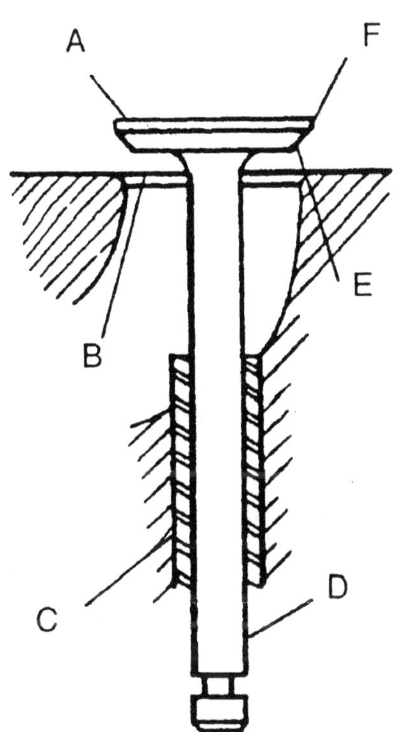


1. Guide 1.____
2. Margin 2.____
3. Seat 3.____
4. Stem 4.____
5. Head 5.____
6. Face 6.____

7. If a rope-rewind starter has a replaceable recoil spring, the FIRST step in replacing it would be to 7.____

A. pull the old spring out as far as possible
B. check the starter for operation
C. release the tension on the old spring
D. disconnect the old spring from the pulley

8. The interface between the primary and secondary circuits in the ignition system is the 8.____

A. magneto
B. condenser
C. breaker points
D. ignition coil

9. Which of the following engine components serves the function of continuing uniform crankshaft motion during all engine actions? 9.____

A. Flywheel
B. Camshaft
C. Governor
D. Main bearing

10. Without obvious misfiring, an engine is observed to lack power. After disconnecting the driven element, the technician should first check for 10.____

A. a dirty air filter
B. fouled ignition points
C. a carbonized combustion chamber
D. frictional loss at the driven element

11. To polarize an internally grounded generator before starting an engine, the ends of the _______ wires should be momentarily touched together. 11.____

A. B and G
B. L and G
C. B and F
D. L and B

12. Which of the following is NOT part of a breather assembly? 12.____

A. Oil trap
B. Bleed port
C. Turbine
D. Check valve

13. Adjustments to governor mechanisms almost always amount to an increase or decrease in 13.____

A. the radius between flyweights and spool
B. the size or mass of flyweights
C. the size of the governor spool
D. governor spring tension

14. Under normal operating conditions, an air filter with a polyurethane outer element and a pleated paper inner element should have the outer element cleaned after every _______ hours of operation. 14.____

A. 10
B. 25
C. 50
D. 100

15. In side-valve engines, valve lash is adjustable by 15.____

A. grinding the cam
B. altering the tappet
C. altering valve spring tension
D. grinding the valve seat or stem end

16. When replacing the rope in a rope-wind starter, the rope should generally be long enough to wind around the flywheel flange pulley _______ times, plus about 6 inches for lead. 16.____

A. 2 to 3 B. 3 to 5 C. 5 to 7 D. 8 to 10

17. Too lean a fuel mixture is most likely to result in 17.____

A. burned valve faces
B. preignition
C. piston damage
D. poor lubrication

18. Whenever possible, which of the following methods for removing an aluminum flywheel should be attempted FIRST? 18.____

A. Lift out with two screwdrivers inserted between the back side of the wheel and the crankcase
B. Heat the hub with a propane torch
C. Use a puller with threads
D. Use a specialized knockoff tool

19. Which of the following problems is LEAST likely to result in the failure of an engine to start? 19.____

A. Corroded battery connection
B. Wrong valve clearance
C. Dirty fuel filter
D. Dirty crankcase breather valve

20. When cleaning a carburetor, the _______ should be removed (except for replacement). 20.____

A. main nozzle
B. throttle plate
C. diaphragm
D. expansion plugs

21. Which of the following steps in cleaning a two-cycle engine should be performed FIRST? 21.____

A. Removing the blower shroud
B. Cleaning the exhaust system
C. Replacing the carburetor air cleaner
D. Removing solvent from the engine surface

22. Which of the following is most likely to cause an engine's fuel mixture to be too rich? 22.____

A. Float set too low
B. Restricted internal air bleed
C. Intake valve sticking closed
D. Clogged float chamber vent

23. The bottom ring on most pistons is the _______ ring. 23.____

A. oil control
B. compression
C. scraper
D. expander

24. Which of the following is considered a normal value (inch) for the radial movement of a small engine flywheel? 24.____

A. 0.002 B. 0.006 C. 0.01 D. 0.03

25. In most carburetors, the high-speed adjustment screw is mounted 25.____

A. on the carburetor body downstream of the low-speed screw
B. under the float bowl
C. downstream of the venturi
D. at the main nozzle

---

# KEY (CORRECT ANSWERS)

1. C
2. D
3. B
4. F
5. A
6. E
7. C
8. D
9. A
10. D
11. C
12. C
13. D
14. B
15. D
16. B
17. A
18. C
19. D
20. C
21. B
22. B
23. A
24. A
25. B

---

# TEST 2

DIRECTIONS: Each question or incomplete statement is followed by several suggested answers or completions. Select the one that BEST answers the question or completes the statement. *PRINT THE LETTER OF THE CORRECT ANSWER IN THE SPACE AT THE RIGHT.*

Questions 1-11.

DIRECTIONS: Questions 1 through 11 refer to the figure below, an exploded view of a starter motor. Place the letter that corresponds to each diagrammed component in the space at the right next to the component's name.

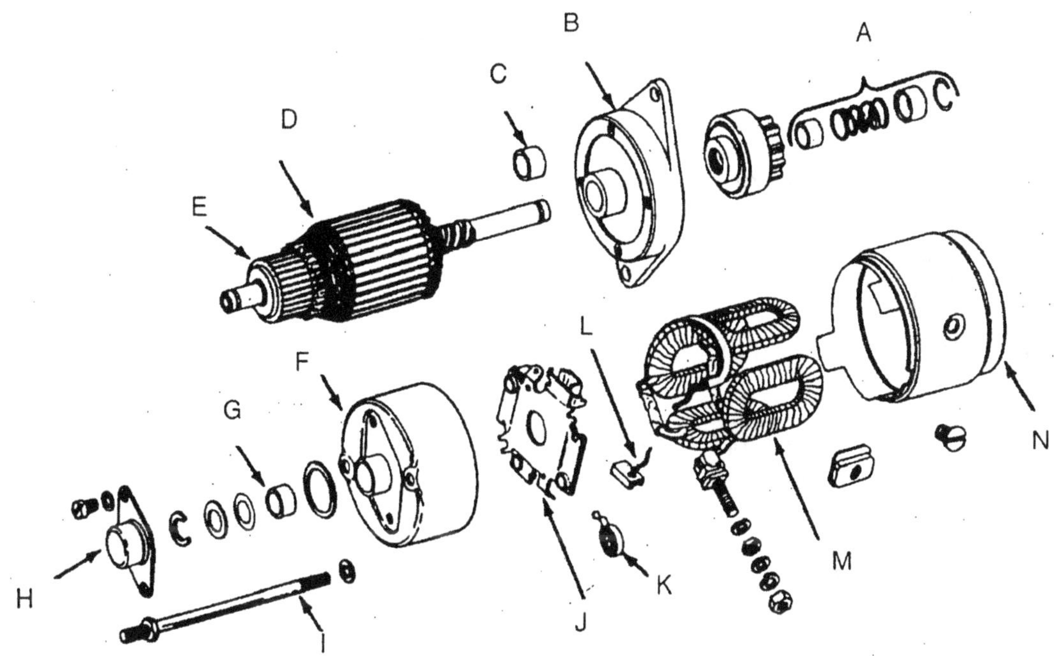


1. Drive-end bushing 1.____
2. Coil 2.____
3. Commutator-end cover plate 3.____
4. Drive assembly 4.____
5. Frame 5.____
6. Brush 6.____
7. Armature 7.____
8. End cap bushing 8.____
9. Brush-holder plate 9.____
10. Commutator 10.____
11. Spring 11.____

12. What is the term for a supporting half-loop of metal, such as one used to hold a glass bowl onto a fuel-filter mount? 12.____

A. Thong  B. Bail  C. Armature  D. Hammock

13. Excessive bearing wear may be caused by 13.____

I. wrong ignition timing
II. a dirty carburetor
III. wrong valve clearance
IV. oil that is too heavy

The CORRECT answer is:

A. I *only*
B. I, IV
C. II, III
D. None of the above

14. A crack on the leading edge of a flywheel keyway suggests that the 14.____

A. crankshaft stopped or suddenly slowed
B. crankshaft was overspeeding the flywheel
C. main bearing is faulty
D. flywheel has become fused to the crankshaft

15. Which of the following symptoms may indicate weak engine valve springs? 15.____

A. Engine knocks
B. Excessive oil consumption (4-cycle)
C. Excessive vibration
D. Misfiring

16. In small engines, any valve guide-to-stem clearance of greater than the maximum _______ inch is considered excessive. 16.____

A. 0.0002  B. 0.0045  C. 0.0025  D. 0.0125

17. An engine kicks back during cranking. The spark output, cooling system, spark plug, PTO adapter, and flywheel are all functioning normally. 17.____
The technician's next step would be to

A. test the ignition coil or spark transformer
B. replace the condenser
C. check the combustion chamber for carbon buildup
D. replace the point set

18. A helicoil is used to 18.____

A. repair stripped bolt threads
B. align magneto magnets
C. remove ridges from the top of cylinder walls
D. clean fouled starter brushes

19. When a magneto fails, the last element that should be suspected as the source of the fault should be the 19.____

A. wiring
B. point contacts
C. coil
D. condenser

20. For side-valve engines, valve lash is measured between the 20.____

    A. valve face and the valve seat when closed
    B. rocker arm and the valve stem
    C. valve face and the valve seat when open
    D. end of the valve stem and the tappet

21. Carburetors fitted to heavy-duty engines usually support the throttle shaft on brass bushings, which should be replaced when side play exceeds ______ inch. 21.____

    A. 0.006 B. 0.002 C. 0.05 D. 0.10

22. A black spark plug insulator tip is a symptom of 22.____

    A. gap bridging
    B. wet fouling
    C. oxide fouling
    D. overheating

23. An engine vibrates excessively, though it is in good tune and the cylinders fire regularly. Generally, the technician should first check the 23.____

    A. crankshaft
    B. driven element
    C. internal engine parts
    D. mounting bolts

24. Usually, intake valve trouble is caused by 24.____

    A. a binding throttle linkage
    B. a broken valve spring
    C. the use of bad gasoline
    D. faulty cooling system

25. If an engine dies when the throttle is closed, the problem is almost certainly 25.____

    A. a binding throttle linkage
    B. overchoking
    C. an obstruction in the low-speed circuit
    D. a misadjusted throttle stop screw

---

# KEY (CORRECT ANSWERS)

1. C
2. M
3. F
4. A
5. N
6. L
7. D
8. G
9. J
10. E
11. K
12. B
13. D
14. B
15. D
16. B
17. A
18. A
19. C
20. D
21. A
22. B
23. D
24. C
25. C

---

# TEST 3

DIRECTIONS: Each question or incomplete statement is followed by several suggested answers or completions. Select the one that BEST answers the question or completes the statement. *PRINT THE LETTER OF THE CORRECT ANSWER IN THE SPACE AT THE RIGHT.*

Questions 1-8.

DIRECTIONS: Questions 1 through 8 refer to the figure below, a view of a Bosch magneto from the power takeoff end. Place the letter that corresponds to each diagrammed component in the space at the right next to the component's name.

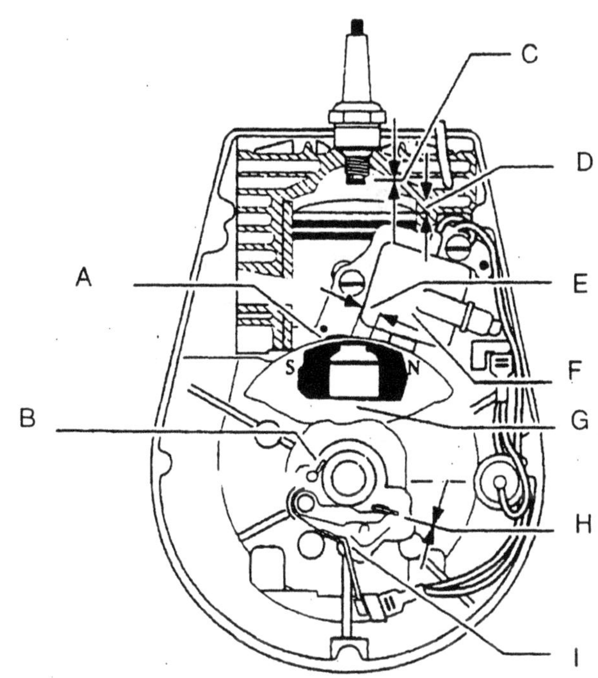


1 Lubricating wick 1.____

2. Coil 2.____

3. Breaker points 3.____

4. Pole shoe break 4.____

5. Flywheel/coil gap 5.____

6. Pole shoe 6.____

7. Ignition setting 7.____

8. Breaker point gap 8.____

9. If the insulator tip of a spark plug is black, then 9.____

   A. the exhaust ports may be clogged
   B. the plug is in the correct heat range
   C. there may be excessive combustion-chamber deposits
   D. the idle adjustment may be too rich

10. If full battery voltage reaches the starter and the flywheel offers normal resistance, but the starter spins without turning the flywheel, which of the following is most likely to be the cause? 10.____

   A. Pinion gear sticking on shaft
   B. Defective armature
   C. Worn shaft bushings
   D. Weak brush springs

11. Magneto open-circuit ignition system voltages generally peak at around _______ volts. 11.____

   A. 7500  B. 12,000  C. 18,000  D. 36,000

12. Which of the following is used to check the specific gravity of a battery? 12.____

   A. Hydrometer  B. Manometer
   C. Ammeter  D. Dynamometer

13. An engine is difficult to start when hot, or often shuts down when running hot. The technician should first check to see if the 13.____

   A. tank and carburetor vents are clean and open
   B. spark plug quality remains constant
   C. choke opens fully
   D. ignition system is operating correctly

14. In ball bearings, the balls are placed in a grooved spacer between the inner and outer 14.____

   A. sleeves  B. races  C. foils  D. jugs

15. On 2-cycle engines, chrome plating is usually most vulnerable to corrosion at 15.____

   A. intake ports  B. the bottom of the bore
   C. the crankcase seal  D. the top of the bore

16. An engine runs, but knocks. It is not overheated or overloaded, all driven elements are tightened, and the flywheel functions normally. The problem is LEAST likely to be 16.____

   A. excessive wear of cylinder bore
   B. loose connecting rod bearings
   C. bad ignition timing
   D. piston wear

17. Which of the following may cause an engine to give off black exhaust? 17.____
   I. Stuck choke
   II. Dirty air cleaner
   III. Flooded engine
   IV. Poor quality fuel

   The CORRECT answer is:

   A. I, II  B. II, III  C. II, III, IV  D. I, II, III, IV

18. Engine stoppage is LEAST likely to be caused by a(n) 18.____

A. improper ignition gap setting
B. defective fuel pump
C. dirty fuel filter
D. blown head gasket

19. If a flywheel is cracked, the cracks will usually appear 19.____

A. radiating inward from the outer edge
B. running longitudinally around the circumference
C. on the fins
D. radiating outward from the keyway

20. Which of the following is evidence of a burned valve? 20.____

A. Weak exhaust back pressure
B. Excessively rich fuel mixture
C. Worn valve retainers
D. Insufficient valve-tappet clearance

21. When re-installing a piston in an integral barrel, which of the following should be done FIRST? 21.____

A. Turning the crankshaft to bottom dead center
B. Positioning the piston as originally found in the engine
C. Installing a compressor tool over the piston
D. Lubricating the cylinder bore

22. Which of the following devices is used to store electrical energy? 22.____

A. Solenoid B. Magneto C. Resistor D. Capacitor

23. Before making external adjustments on a carburetor, the engine should be run for a minimum of______ minute(s). 23.____

A. 1 B. 5 C. 10 D. 15

24. Which of the following ignition system problems may cause a backfire at the carburetor? 24.____

A. Wrong timing
B. Wrong spark plug gap
C. Worn points
D. Bad ignition coil

25. Which of the following is NOT a symptom that might indicate a bent crankshaft? 25.____

A. Crankshaft drags when turned by hand
B. Crankshaft locked
C. Crankshaft alternately binds and releases during cranking
D. Misfires

# KEY (CORRECT ANSWERS)

1. B
2. F
3. I
4. E
5. A
6. G
7. D
8. H
9. D
10. A
11. C
12. A
13. C
14. B
15. D
16. C
17. D
18. C
19. D
20. D
21. A
22. D
23. D
24. A
25. D

# EXAMINATION SECTION
# TEST 1

DIRECTIONS: Each question or incomplete statement is followed by several suggested answers or completions. Select the one that BEST answers the question or completes the statement. *PRINT THE LETTER OF THE CORRECT ANSWER IN THE SPACE AT THE RIGHT.*

Questions 1-10.

DIRECTIONS: Questions 1 through 10 refer to the figure below, a cutaway view of a diaphragm carburetor. Place the letter that corresponds to each diagrammed component in the space at the right next to the component's name.

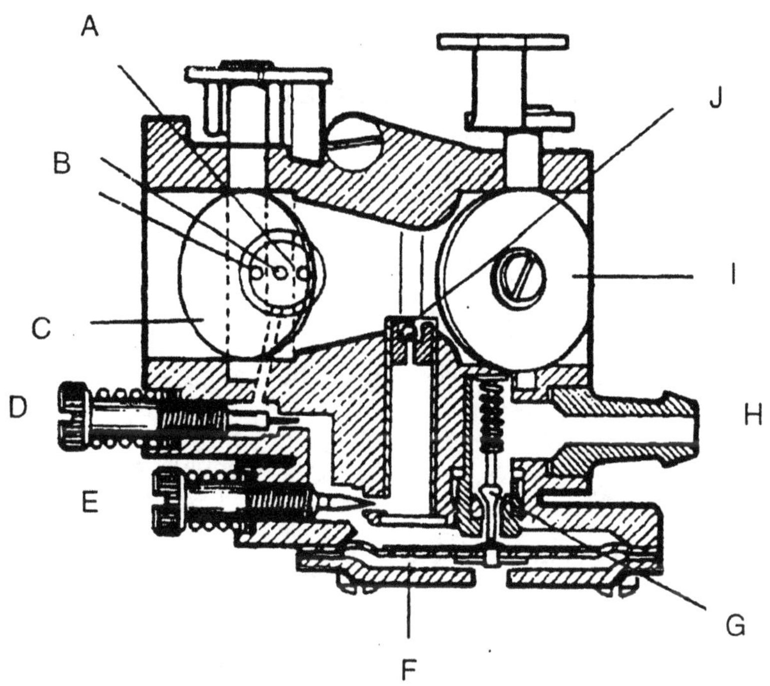


1. Idle adjust 1.____
2. Diaphragm 2.____
3. Inlet needle and seat 3.____
4. Air bleed 4.____
5. Choke shutter 5.____
6. Idle and intermediate ports 6.____
7. Ball check 7.____
8. Main adjust 8.____
9. Throttle shutter 9.____
10. Fuel inlet 10.____

11. Which of the following terms is sometimes used to describe the act of removing burned gases from the cylinder after a working stroke? 11.____

A. Blow-by
B. Scavenging
C. Shrouding
D. Scrubbing

12. Which of the following is NOT considered to be a purpose of a crankcase breather assembly? 12.____

A. Keeping a partial vacuum in the crankcase
B. Keeping the fuel mixture consistent
C. Removing harmful vapors from the crankcase
D. Keeping out dust and dirt

13. When replacing a spark plug, it is common practice to 13.____

A. clean the socket thoroughly before installation
B. replace it with the wire in place
C. burnish the point of the new plug
D. turn it 3 revolutions by hand before applying a wrench

14. Multicylinder engines universally time their ignition to the number ______ cylinder. 14.____

A. 1
B. 2
C. 3
D. 4

15. If an engine's rpm tend to rise and fall when it is held at half-throttle, the most likely cause is a 15.____

A. hunting governor
B. misadjusted idle screw
C. clogged pickup tube
D. bound throttle linkage

16. Most starter problems originate with the 16.____

A. bushings
B. commutator
C. brushes
D. armature

17. Which of the following is considered a normal value (inch) for the axial movement of a small engine flywheel? 17.____

A. 0.002
B. 0.006
C. 0.01
D. 0.03

18. An engine's rewind starter fails to engage the flywheel. The most likely cause is a 18.____

A. worn or distorted brake spring
B. broken main spring
C. broken dog
D. bad alignment between the starter housing and the flywheel

19. Most modern ignition systems used for small engines are open circuits that deliver ______ volts. 19.____

A. 10,000
B. 25,000
C. 50,000
D. 100,000

20. In 2-cycle engines, an improper oil-to-fuel ratio is most likely to cause 20.____

A. wet fouling of spark plugs
B. overheated plugs
C. dry fouling of spark plugs
D. gap bridging of plug electrodes

21. What is the term for a rotating machine part supported in a bearing? 21.____

A. Traverse B. Journal C. Sleeve D. Shaft

22. Which of the following exists only in the crankcase of a 4-cycle engine? 22.____

A. Camshaft
B. Bottom of piston
C. Crankshaft
D. Connecting rod

23. Which of the following is NOT an aspect of connecting rod orientation? 23.____

A. Rod-to-bore
B. Piston-to-rod
C. Cap-to-rod
D. Rod assembly-to-engine

24. Which of the following should be used to check whether a starter generator is working properly? 24.____

A. Ohmmeter
B. Voltmeter
C. Dynamometer
D. Ammeter

25. Thrust bearings in small engines are normally present as 25.____

A. a bushing over the top end of the crankshaft
B. rollers at the end of the camshaft
C. a hardened washer at the top end of the crankshaft
D. sleeves over the ends of the governor shaft

---

# KEY (CORRECT ANSWERS)

1. D
2. F
3. G
4. A
5. I
6. B
7. J
8. E
9. C
10. H
11. B
12. B
13. D
14. A
15. A
16. C
17. B
18. A
19. C
20. D
21. B
22. A
23. A
24. D
25. C

# TEST 2

DIRECTIONS: Each question or incomplete statement is followed by several suggested answers or completions. Select the one that BEST answers the question or completes the statement. *PRINT THE LETTER OF THE CORRECT ANSER IN THE SPACE AT THE RIGHT.*

1. Which of the following are likely to cause cylinder wear? 1.____
   I. Dirty crankcase breather valve
   II. Dirty air cleaner
   III. Low oil level
   IV. Dirty carburetor

   The CORRECT answer is:

   A. I, II B. II, III
   C. III, IV D. I, III, IV

2. In troubleshooting an ignition system, a technician's last resort should be to check the 2.____

   A. flywheel B. timing C. coil D. points

3. What is the piston displacement (cubic inches) of a one-cylinder engine with a bore of 2 inches and a stroke of 2 inches? 3.____

   A. 4.65 B. 5.04 C. 6.28 D. 8.75

4. What is the term for the removable cylinder barrels used in 2-cycle engines? 4.____

   A. Sheaves B. Bores C. Sleeves D. Jugs

5. When testing a 12-volt DC starter circuit, a technician closes the starter switch. The voltage drops below 10 volts. 5.____
   Most likely, this indicates that

   A. the system has a poor ground connection
   B. there is a poor connection between the battery and the starter switch
   C. the starter switch is not closing the circuit properly
   D. the starter motor is faulty

6. On engines with relatively large flywheels, which of the following is LEAST likely to be the cause of a spontaneous loss of timing in the ignition system? 6.____

   A. Sheared or deformed key
   B. Loose PTO
   C. Wallowed keyway
   D. Loose flywheel retaining nut

7. Which of the following may be caused by a blown head gasket? 7.____
   I. Piston ring wear
   II. Governor hunting
   III. Overheating (water cooled engines)
   IV. Knocking

   The CORRECT answer is:

   A. I, III B. II, IV C. III *only* D. III, IV

8. An engine's crankcase breather is passing oil. Which of the following is most likely to be the cause? 8._____

   A. Worn main bearings
   B. Scored crankshaft
   C. Piston ring gaps aligned
   D. Breather valve stuck closed

9. Which of the following is NOT a common cause of badly burned contact points in magneto ignition systems? 9._____

   A. Oil or foreign material on contact surfaces
   B. Worn cam lobe
   C. Out-of-adjustment point gap
   D. A defective condenser

10. Despite a clean fuel supply, a cranking speed of 90 rpm, and a clean air filter, an engine does not start. Checks reveal that the spark plugs are dry and the choke functions normally. 10._____
    The next check should be at the

    A. carburetor air horn
    B. valve timing
    C. fuel line
    D. throttle

11. If a spark plug's electrodes are worn, then 11._____

    A. the engine is overloaded
    B. there is excessive carbon in the cylinder
    C. the idle speed is too low
    D. the plugs are requiring more voltage to fire

12. In adjusting the breaker-point timing of a magneto with a continuity tester, which of the following is usually done FIRST? 12._____

    A. Rotating crankshaft by hand until timing marks are aligned
    B. Connecting the continuity tester to a ground
    C. Loosening the breaker-point lock screw
    D. Disconnecting the primary-coil lead wire at the terminal stud

13. Which of the following is used to prevent the flywheel from turning while the flywheel nut is loosened? 13._____

    A. Impact nut
    B. Torque wrench
    C. Rolling tool
    D. Chain wrench

14. In a carburetor, a failure of the throttle plate to close can be caused by each of the following EXCEPT 14._____

    A. the idle rpm being set too high
    B. a misadjusted throttle cable
    C. a malfunctioning governor
    D. overpriming

15. A crankshaft alternately binds and releases during cranking. Which of the following is LEAST likely to be the cause? 15.____

A. Incorrect valve timing
B. Misaligned flywheel
C. Hydraulic lock
D. Loose blade (mowers)

16. With contacts closed, the interlock of a small engine's ignition system should have a resistance of _______ ohms. 16.____

A. 0
B. 50
C. 100
D. Infinity

17. Which of the following may cause wear on the connecting rod? 17.____

I. Dirty crankcase breather valve
II. Oil level too low
III. Wrong bearing clearance
IV. Blown head gasket

The CORRECT answer is:

A. I, II
B. II, III
C. I, II, III
D. II, III, IV

18. Mechanical governors generally sense engine speed as 18.____

A. flyweight movement
B. fuel intake velocity
C. spark intervals
D. throttle angle

19. If carbon deposits are discovered on a valve face, each of the following is a likely cause EXCEPT 19.____

A. high seating impact from excessive valve-tappet clearance
B. worn valve guides
C. loose valve seat insert
D. excessive valve spring tension

20. Most magneto faults originate in the 20.____

A. coil
B. breaker points
C. point spring
D. condenser

21. Sticking is a problem that occurs most often with _______ valves. 21.____

A. exhaust
B. intake
C. breather
D. reed

22. Which of the following is NOT a typical cause of engine knock? 22.____

A. Loose PTO adapter
B. Worn cylinder bore
C. Carbon buildup in combustion chamber
D. Worn valve guides

23. Which of the following may be caused by a dirty air filter? 23.____

I. Piston ring wear
II. Misfiring
III. Knocking
IV. Governor hunting

The CORRECT answer is:

A. I *only*
B. I, II
C. II, III
D. III, IV

24. Which of the following is used to perform electronic switching and amplification functions? 24.____

A. Venturi
B. Transistor
C. Resistor
D. Diode

25. A properly-honed cylinder bore should appear to have a fine ______ pattern of scratches. 25.____

A. spiraling
B. longitudinal
C. cross-hatched
D. horizontal

---

# KEY (CORRECT ANSWERS)

1. B
2. B
3. C
4. D
5. A

6. B
7. C
8. C
9. B
10. C

11. D
12. A
13. D
14. D
15. C

16. A
17. C
18. A
19. B
20. B

21. A
22. D
23. B
24. B
25. C

---

# TEST 3

DIRECTIONS: Each question or incomplete statement is followed by several suggested answers or completions. Select the one that BEST answers the question or completes the statement. *PRINT THE LETTER OF THE CORRECT ANSWER IN THE SPACE AT THE RIGHT.*

Questions 1-8.

DIRECTIONS: Questions 1 through 8 refer to the figure below, an exploded view of a retractable rope starter. Place the letter that corresponds to each diagrammed component in the space at the right next to the component's name.

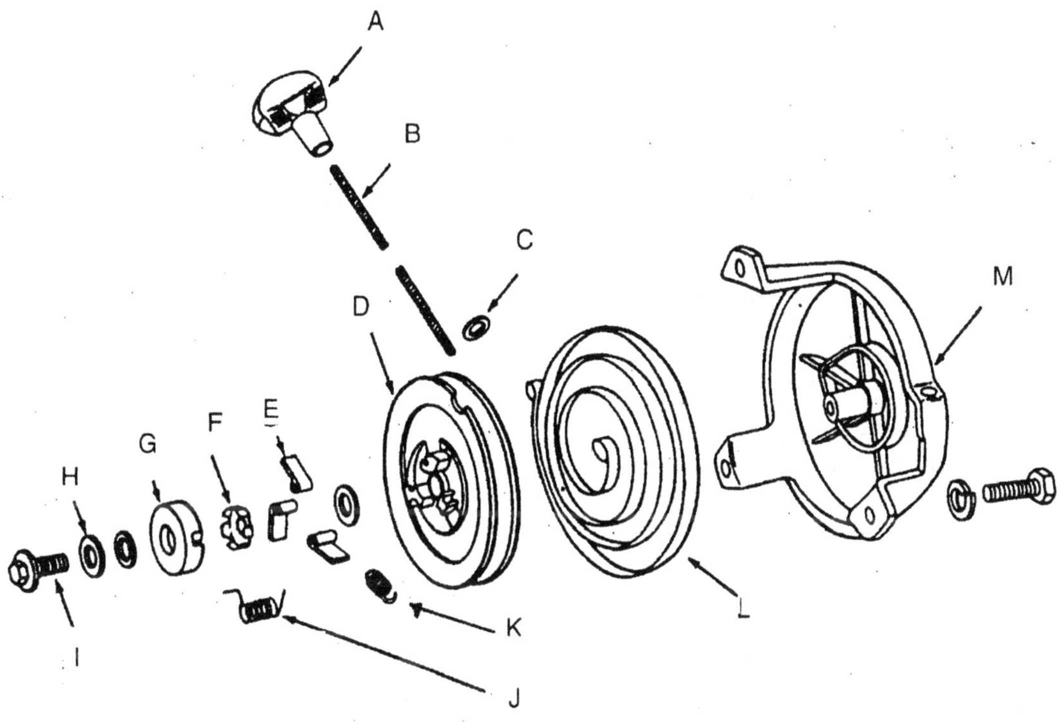


1. Pulley 1.____
2. Rewind spring 2.____
3. Dog retainer 3.____
4. Retainer spring 4.____
5. Capscrew 5.____
6. Spring brake 6.____
7. Dog 7.____
8. Dog tension spring 8.____

9. What is the term for a narrow passage that causes a low pressure at the area in the air passage that is just beyond the narrowed portion? 9.____

A. Venturi B. Cyclone C. Vortex D. Turbine

10. If an engine experiences a loss of power, which of the following is LEAST likely to be the cause? 10.____

A. Incorrect valve timing
B. Worn valve guides
C. Leaking crankcase seals (2-cycle)
D. Restricted exhaust ports (2-cycle)

11. Small engines generally require a minimum cranking compression of ______ psi in order to start. 11.____

A. 40 B. 60 C. 80 D. 100

12. A technician is testing a faulty starting circuit. All terminals are clean and tight, the battery cables are in good condition, and the battery is adequately charged.
The test reveals that there is no voltage from the ignition switch *start* terminal to the solenoid. The next step for the technician would be to 12.____

A. replace the starter motor
B. check the incoming voltage at the ignition switch
C. replace the defective solenoid
D. trace the circuit back to the ignition switch

13. An overheated spark plug may be indicated by 13.____

A. a carbon layer over the entire nose
B. a light gray insulator tip
C. deposits between electrodes
D. an oily film over the firing end

14. An engine's flywheel does not turn with its starter. After disabling the ignition, the technician sees that the driven element is not obstructed, and yet it does not move if turned by hand. The next step should be to 14.____

A. repair the starting system
B. remove the spark plugs
C. drain all fluids from the cylinder
D. replace the governor

15. A technician is testing a charging circuit that uses a rectifier. The battery is charged, the voltage is normal with the engine shut down, but the running voltage is high. The next step should be to 15.____

A. replace the rectifier
B. disconnect the AC output leads to the rectifier
C. run a controlled load (e.g., headlamps) on the battery with the engine stopped
D. replace the stator

16. After 16 hours on the charger, the potential of a nicad battery should range between _______ V. 16._____

A. 4.5 to 7.5
B. 9.5 to 12.5
C. 13.5 to 15
D. 15.5 to 18

17. If full battery voltage reaches the starter and the flywheel offers normal resistance but the starter works only intermittently, each of the following may be the cause EXCEPT 17._____

A. dirty commutator
B. loose connections in external circuit
C. worn shaft bushings
D. sticking brushes

18. In diagnosing the ignition system of a small engine, a technician finds that the external ignition circuit is functioning normally, but the system is not delivering a spark. The ignition switch, interlocks, battery, and spark plug are known to be functioning normally. The next step would be to 18._____

A. check the flywheel and keyways
B. burnish the contact points
C. check the distributor cap and rotor
D. replace the condenser

19. Which of the following is a symptom that is most likely to indicate a bent crankshaft? 19._____

A. Excessive vibration
B. Loss of power
C. Engine knocking
D. Crankcase breather passes oil

20. In 2-cycle engines, failure of the crankcase to hold pressure is almost always the fault of the 20._____

A. pump or dipper
B. crankcase breather
C. piston ring gaps
D. crankshaft seals

21. An engine runs, but knocks. It is not overheated or overloaded. The first check for trouble should be at the 21._____

A. PTO coupling or blade adapter
B. piston or cylinder bore
C. flywheel
D. ignition timing

22. Under normal conditions, a spark plug's insulator tip will appear 22._____

A. light gray or chalky white
B. black
C. pale blue
D. brown to light tan

23. Within the carburetor, the transition between low- and high-speed circuits generally occurs at about _______ throttle. 23._____

A. 1/4
B. 1/2
C. 3/4
D. full

24. If an engine stumbles under load, each of the following is a probable cause EXCEPT 24.____

A. improper valve clearance
B. leaking crankcase seal (2-cycle)
C. weak valve springs
D. faulty breather

25. When testing the ignition system of most small engines, the flywheel should be spun at the normal cranking speed of approximately ______ rpm. 25.____

A. 50 B. 100 C. 150 D. 300

---

# KEY (CORRECT ANSWERS)

1. D
2. L
3. G
4. K
5. I

6. F
7. E
8. J
9. A
10. B

11. B
12. D
13. B
14. B
15. A

16. D
17. C
18. A
19. A
20. D

21. A
22. D
23. A
24. D
25. C

---

# EXAMINATION SECTION
# TEST 1

DIRECTIONS: Each question or incomplete statement is followed by several suggested answers or completions. Select the one that BEST answers the question or completes the statement. *PRINT THE LETTER OF THE CORRECT ANSWER IN THE SPACE AT THE RIGHT.*

1. A typical small engine generates about ______ psi of compression at normal cranking speeds. 1.____

   A. 40-60 B. 80-100 C. 100-150 D. 150-200

2. If full battery voltage reaches the starter and the flywheel offers normal resistance but the starter cranks slowly, each of the following may be a cause EXCEPT 2.____

   A. defective armature
   B. worn shaft bushings
   C. worn brushes
   D. grounded field coil

3. Which of the following is a device for transposing rotary motion into an alternating reciprocating motion? 3.____

   A. Connecting rod
   B. Piston
   C. Differential
   D. Cam

4. Which of the following is most likely to cause engine overheating? 4.____

   A. Valve-guide distortion
   B. Restricted exhaust system
   C. Scored cylinder walls
   D. Worn piston rings

5. Which of the following is NOT a term used to describe the relationship between an ignition coil armature and the magneto magnet at the moment of point break? 5.____

   A. Pole shoe break
   B. Breakaway gap
   C. Wallow
   D. Edge distance

6. Capacitance is measured in 6.____

   A. amps
   B. horsepower
   C. farads
   D. ohms

7. Which of the following is a symptom that might indicate a jammed starter drive? 7.____

   A. Crankshaft alternately binds and releases
   B. Dragging crankshaft when turned by hand
   C. Rough idle
   D. Locked crankshaft

8. An ignition system delivers an erratic spark. After a technician checks the ignition switch, battery, interlocks, and spark plug, he or she should 8.____

   A. change the point set
   B. inspect the flywheel and keyways
   C. check the spark plug lead
   D. check the external ignition circuit with an ohmmeter

9. Which of the following would be a normal value for crank-case compression in a 2-cycle engine during cranking? 9.____

A. 5 B. 10 C. 30 D. 60

10. In small engines, engine faults usually originate in the ______ system. 10.____

A. ignition B. electrical
C. fuel D. mechanical

11. The use of nonrecommended oils may cause 11.____

A. the insulator tip of a spark plug to be choked with ash-like deposits
B. a carbon layer over the entire nose of the plug
C. worn spark plug electrodes
D. wet fouling

12. Which of the following steps in the operation of a capacitive discharge ignition (CDI) system occurs FIRST? 12.____

A. A large voltage is generated in the transformer secondary winding.
B. The silicon-controlled rectifier becomes conductive.
C. The rectifier converts alternating current to direct current.
D. The magnet passes the trigger coil.

13. Which of the following would be used to test a condenser? 13.____

A. Ammeter B. Ohmmeter
C. Voltmeter D. Dynamometer

14. What is the term for the linear distance between the shell gasket of a spark plug and the end of the threaded portion of the shell? 14.____

A. Cleft B. Gap C. Trace D. Reach

15. The control loop of a small engine's starter circuit begins with a length of ______ -gauge wire from the positive battery terminal. 15.____

A. 10 B. 14 C. 18 D. 22

16. In most situations, a spontaneous loss of engine timing appears to be limited to ignition systems which ______ the flywheel. 16.____

A. cluster all parts beneath
B. have a coil mounted outside
C. receive their firing impulses from
D. receive their firing impulses from a rotor mounted under

17. Which of the following is LEAST likely to be a cause of engine failure? 17.____

A. Blocked air cleaners and cooling fins
B. Electrical fault
C. Operating under load for too long
D. Improper lubrication

18. Despite a clean fuel supply, a cranking speed of 90 rpm, and a clean air filter, an engine does not start. The first check should be made at the 18.____

A. muffler B. choke C. fuel line D. spark plug

19. A crow's foot tool may be used to 19.____

A. reattach piston pin circlips
B. collapse valve springs during removal
C. rotate a piston ring into place
D. ream a valve guide

20. In adjusting the point gap of a magneto, which of the following should typically be done FIRST? 20.____

A. Burnish the contact faces
B. Lightly snug the hold-down screw
C. Move the stationary point
D. Turn the flywheel until the points open

21. While inspecting the starter, a technician observes a ring of solder thrown against the inside of the housing. This indicates that the 21.____

A. brushes are worn
B. armature bearings are worn
C. commutator is out of round
D. starter is overheating

22. What is the horsepower of an engine that is capable of lifting 200 pounds to a height of 55 feet in 10 seconds? 22.____

A. 1.5 B. 2 C. 2.8 D. 4.2

23. Which of the following is a device that changes alternating current into direct current? 23.____

A. Capacitor B. Rectifier
C. Transistor D. Magneto

24. When using a drill press to hone a bore, it is important to remember that a maximum of _______ rpm should be used in order to avoid threading. 24.____

A. 250 B. 400 C. 800 D. 1200

25. Which of the following is NOT a fuel-regulating mechanism used in small-engine carburetors? 25.____

A. Diaphragm B. Shutter
C. Float D. Pickup tube

# KEY (CORRECT ANSWERS)

1. B
2. D
3. D
4. B
5. C

6. C
7. D
8. D
9. A
10. A

11. A
12. C
13. B
14. D
15. B

16. C
17. B
18. D
19. B
20. B

21. D
22. B
23. B
24. B
25. B

---

# TEST 2

DIRECTIONS: Each question or incomplete statement is followed by several suggested answers or completions. Select the one that BEST answers the question or completes the statement. *PRINT THE LETTER OF THE CORRECT ANSWER IN THE SPACE AT THE RIGHT.*

1. Approximately what percentage of the heat generated by fuel combustion is used to develop power? 1.____

   A. 1/5 B. 1/3 C. 1/2 D. 2/3

2. What is the term for an automatic switch in the primary circuit of an engine that shuts down the ignition under unsafe operating conditions? 2.____

   A. Trip B. Interlock C. Safety D. Knockout

3. The most commonly used spark gap for small engine plugs is ______ inch. 3.____

   A. 0.010 B. 0.015 C. 0.025 D. 0.066

4. An engine is consuming oil at an excessive rate. Each of the following is a probable cause EXCEPT 4.____

   A. worn cylinder bore
   B. worn valve guides
   C. faulty breather
   D. loss of compression

5. Battery capacity is typically expressed in terms of 5.____

   A. ampere-hours
   B. volts
   C. foot-candles
   D. volt-hours

6. In oil systems using a slinger, the slinger is driven by the 6.____

   A. cam gear
   B. connecting rod
   C. crankshaft
   D. oil pump

7. The drawbacks associated with crossflow scavenging, a feature of some two-cycle engines, include each of the following EXCEPT 7.____

   A. piston heavy and prone to distortion
   B. dilution of fuel mixture by exhaust gases
   C. reed valve prone to scorching
   D. loss of unburnt fuel in exhaust

8. Too rich a fuel mixture may result in 8.____

   A. burned valve seats
   B. sticking valve stems
   C. hot rings
   D. carbon deposits in the engine

9. In float-type carburetors, flooding is likely to occur if the 9.____

   A. float bowl vent is clogged
   B. float is set too high
   C. needle sticks
   D. needle fails to seal against the inlet seat

10. In aligning the starter clutch and the flywheel hub of an engine, which of the following should be done FIRST? 10.____

A. Attaching the starter housing assembly loosely to the engine
B. Tightening the starter hold-down screws
C. Cycling the starter a few times
D. Pulling the starter handle out about 8 inches

11. For most battery and coil ignition systems, the point gap should be a tight _______ inch. 11.____

A. 0.006 B. 0.010 C. 0.020 D. 0.25

12. In conventional small engine ignition systems, a thick _______ spark is delivered. 12.____

A. yellow B. white C. red D. blue

13. If full battery voltage reaches the starter and the flywheel offers normal resistance but the starter does not function, each of the following may be a cause EXCEPT 13.____

A. brushes stuck in holder
B. open armature
C. oily commutator
D. defective field coil

14. A lead-acid battery should be discarded if a charger cannot raise average cell readings to at least 14.____

A. 0.800 B. 1.080 C. 1.260 D. 1.840

15. A technician is testing a faulty starting circuit. All terminals are clean and tight, the battery cables are in good condition, and the battery is adequately charged. The next step for the technician should be to 15.____

A. connect a jumper cable across the solenoid cable terminals
B. measure the control voltage at the solenoid with the ignition switch on
C. check the incoming voltage at the ignition switch
D. replace the starter motor

16. In a two-cycle engine, too much oil in the mixture is likely to cause each of the following problems EXCEPT 16.____

A. shortened spark plug life
B. accelerated cylinder bore wear
C. difficult starting
D. lowered fuel octane reading

17. The rectifier of a small engine's starter circuit has been determined to be defective. The FIRST step in replacing would be to 17.____

A. remove the flywheel
B. disconnect the leads to the rectifier
C. remove the stator
D. remove the rectifier

18. Utility engines, especially those with splash lubrication systems, require a minimum of _______ rpm idle speed to assure oil circulation. 18.____

A. 1000 B. 1600 C. 2200 D. 3000

19. On nicad batteries, a white powder appearing on cells indicates 19.____

A. cadmium leakage
B. nickel deposits
C. condensation
D. oxidation

20. Normally-functioning ignition systems will produce a pulse of high-voltage electrical energy timed to occur as the piston 20.____

A. nears bottom dead center
B. nears top dead center
C. is traveling upward midway through the bore
D. is traveling downward midway through the bore

21. The best and most cost-effective air filters used with small engines are usually made of 21.____

A. paper fiber throughout
B. polyurethane throughout
C. a polyurethane outer element with a pleated paper inner element
D. gauze of fiber

22. Which of the following symptoms might indicate a stuck breather valve? 22.____

A. Engine knocks
B. Loss of power
C. No crankcase compression (2-cycle)
D. Rough idle

23. Most small-engine valve margins measure about _______ inch. 23.____

A. 1/64 B. 1/32 C. 1/16 D. 1/8

24. Which of the following is a device that reverses the direction of electric current in any circuit? 24.____

A. Alternator
B. Condenser
C. Commutator
D. Magneto

25. The purpose of pawls in a rope-rewind assembly is to 25.____

A. initiate the recoil
B. turn the starter pulley
C. keep the rope from coming loose
D. engage the crankshaft adapter

---

# KEY (CORRECT ANSWERS)

1. B
2. B
3. C
4. D
5. A
6. A
7. C
8. D
9. D
10. A
11. C
12. D
13. D
14. C
15. A
16. B
17. B
18. B
19. A
20. B
21. C
22. D
23. A
24. C
25. D

# TEST 3

DIRECTIONS: Each question or incomplete statement is followed by several suggested answers or completions. Select the one that BEST answers the question or completes the statement. *PRINT THE LETTER OF THE CORRECT ANSWER IN THE SPACE AT THE RIGHT.*

Questions 1-14.

DIRECTIONS: Questions 1 through 14 refer to the figure below, a cutaway diagram of a simple single-cylinder, air-cooled four-cycle engine. Place the letter that corresponds to each diagrammed component in the space at the right next to the component's name.

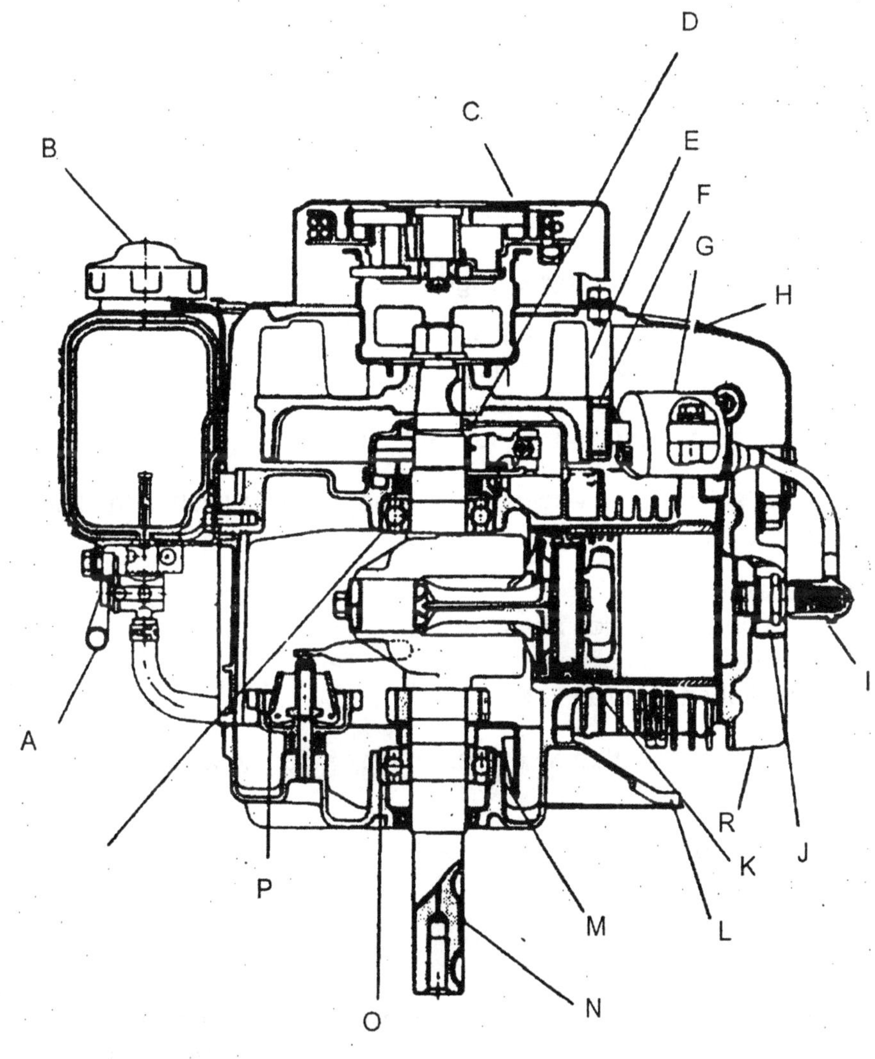


1. Magneto breaker points 1.____

2. Spark plug cap 2.____

3. Air shroud 3.____

4. Flywheel 4.____

5. Piston pin 5.____

6. Fuel shutoff valve and strainer 6.____

7. Crankshaft 7.____

8. Oil dipper 8.____

9. Ignition coil 9.____

10. Recoil starter 10.____

11. Spark plug 11.____

12. Flyweight governor 12.____

13. Magneto magnet 13.____

14. Gear cover 14.____

15. The purpose of a reed valve of two-cycle engines is to 15.____

    A. expel blow-by gases from the combustion chamber
    B. admit fuel into the combustion chamber
    C. admit air into the combustion chamber
    D. admit fuel from the carburetor into the crankcase

16. Oil is observed to be leaking at an engine's crankshaft seals. Which of the following is MOST likely to be the cause? 16.____

    A. Worn main bearings
    B. Carbon buildup in combustion chamber
    C. Clogged oil-drain holes in piston
    D. Excessive crankshaft endplay

17. An engine fails to run at a large throttle angle. Which of the following is LEAST likely to be the cause? 17.____

    A. Weak throttle springs
    B. Binding throttle shaft
    C. Misadjusted throttle stop screw
    D. Failed governor

18. A technician tests a faulty battery and coil ignition system and discovers that the primary voltage is present at the movable point arm with contacts open, and absent with the points closed. Most likely, the problem is in the 18.____

    A. secondary circuit B. ignition switch
    C. battery D. ground

19. Most starting circuit problems are the fault of the 19.____

    A. battery B. solenoid
    C. starter motor D. ignition switch

20. A technician is testing an AC charging circuit with a 6V battery with the engine running near the governed maximum speed. Which of the following voltage readings would fall within the normal range? 20.____

A. 4.5 B. 6 C. 10 D. 12

21. The use of knockoff tools is LEAST likely to do damage when removing flywheels that have a______ main bearing. 21.____

A. ball B. roller C. sleeve D. needle

22. Which of the following may cause an engine to give off blue exhaust? 22.____

A. Dirty carburetor
B. Wrong bearing clearance
C. Stuck choke
D. Worn piston rings

23. To burnish magneto points for the purpose of removing oil, oxidation, or fingerprints, a technican should use 23.____

A. a mild acid solution
B. cardboard
C. steel wool
D. an emery cloth

24. The cranking voltage of a 12V battery should remain above ______ V. 24.____

A. 4.5 B. 6.5 C. 9.5 D. 12.5

25. Assume that an engine has a no-load speed of 1800 RPM and a full-load speed of 1650 RPM.
The speed regulation of this engine is MOST NEARLY 25.____

A. 12% B. 11% C. 9.1% D. 8.4%

---

# KEY (CORRECT ANSWERS)

1. D
2. I
3. H
4. E
5. K
6. A
7. N
8. M
9. G
10. C
11. J
12. P
13. F
14. L
15. D
16. A
17. C
18. A
19. A
20. B
21. C
22. D
23. B
24. C
25. C

---

# TEST 4

DIRECTIONS: Each question or incomplete statement is followed by several suggested answers or completions. Select the one that BEST answers the question or completes the statement. *PRINT THE LETTER OF THE CORRECT ANSWER IN THE SPACE AT THE RIGHT.*

1. Which of the following is NOT an element of the carburetor's high-speed circuit? 1.____

   A. Idle jet
   B. Main jet
   C. Interconnecting passages
   D. Fuel nozzle

2. Each of the following is a common type of fuel screen used in small engine systems EXCEPT a(n) 2.____

   A. inline filter screen in the carburetor
   B. screen in the fuel tank attached to the fuel shut-off valve
   C. screen in the fuel tank over the fill opening
   D. strainer attached to the end of a fuel pickup hose in the tank

3. Which of the following creates the electromagnetic effect in a motor such as a starting motor? 3.____

   A. Servo
   B. Coil
   C. Diode
   D. Commutator

4. Which throttle/governor system problem is most likely to result in the failure of an engine to start? 4.____

   A. Linkage binding
   B. Linkage worn or disconnected
   C. Linkage out of adjustment
   D. Governor spring sensitivity too great

5. In non-CDI ignition systems, a generating magnet can be considered functional if it attracts a loosely-held screwdriver through an air gap of at LEAST ______ inch(es). 5.____

   A. 1/4 B. 3/4 C. 1 D. 1 1/2

6. In 4-cycle engines, the intake and exhaust valves are both closed during the ______ stroke. 6.____

   I. intake
   II. compression
   III. power
   IV. exhaust

   The CORRECT answer is:

   A. I, III B. II, IV C. II, III D. III, IV

7. An engine is observed to experience sudden surges in power. The fuel supply is known to be clean. The next step for a technician would generally be to check the 7.____

   A. throttle linkage
   B. tank vent
   C. carburetor adjustment
   D. ignition system

8. A technician is testing a 10-amp alternator system after discovering an insufficient charge in the battery. After disconnecting the positive battery lead, the technician checks the voltage between the battery lead and the ground at full throttle. The reading is about 6 volts.
Which of the following is indicated? The 8.____

   A. regulator is defective
   B. throttle is sticking
   C. stator is defective
   D. problem is with the battery

9. An engine gives off black smoke and a wet exhaust. Which of the following is LEAST likely to be a cause? 9.____

   A. Partially closed choke
   B. Misadjusted jets
   C. Restricted air cleaner
   D. Binding throttle linkage

10. Which of the following mechanical components is LEAST likely to wear in a 4-cycle engine? 10.____

   A. Piston
   B. Piston ring
   C. Cylinder
   D. Wrist pin bearing

11. Which of the following is NOT considered to be a symptom of magneto coil failure? 11.____

   A. Misfiring
   B. No or low spark voltage
   C. Popback through the carburetor
   D. Intermittent voltage output

12. The crankcase breather assembly can usually be located 12.____

   A. at the end of the crankshaft
   B. over the drain plug
   C. at the bottom of the cylinder bore
   D. in the valve tappet access well

13. The spark output, cooling system, and spark plug of a small engine are known to be in good condition, but the engine kicks back during cranking. The first thing a technician should check is the 13.____

   A. ignition coil
   B. PTO adapter
   C. condenser
   D. flywheel

14. Which of the following steps in removing a side valve is performed FIRST? 14.____

   A. Compressing the valve spring
   B. Inserting the compressor into the valve collar
   C. Remove valve locks
   D. Rotating the flywheel to seat the valve

15. The cylinder head of a small engine is considered to be flush if a feeler gauge no thicker than _______ inch can be passed between the bolt holes. 15.____

   A. 0.009 B. 0.003 C. 0.025 D. 0.010

16. The FIRST step in making ignition timing adjustments should always be to 16.____

    A. connect a test lamp across the points
    B. locate the timing marks
    C. set the breaker point gap to manufacturer's specifications
    D. bring the piston up on the compression stroke

17. Which of the following is most likely to cause an engine's fuel mixture to be too lean? 17.____

    A. Float set too high
    B. Restricted internal air bleed
    C. Intake valve sticking open
    D. Clogged float chamber vent

18. Each of the following is a symptom of ignition system condenser failure EXCEPT 18.____

    A. misfires
    B. decreased breaker point arcing
    C. reduced spark output
    D. migration of tungsten from one point face to another

19. For overhead-valve engines, valve lash is measured between the 19.____

    A. valve face and the valve seat when closed
    B. rocker arm and the valve stem
    C. valve face and the valve seat when open
    D. end of the valve stem and the tappet

20. A lean carburetor setting may cause 20.____

    A. a carbon layer over the entire nose of the plug
    B. a damp oily film over the firing end of the spark plu
    C. a choked insulator tip
    D. burned spark plug electrodes

21. Which of the following steps in checking engine compression should be performed FIRST? 21.____

    A. Checking for cylinder head trouble
    B. Giving the flywheel a quick twist
    C. Disconnecting the spark plug wire
    D. Checking for dry piston rings and cylinder walls

22. Which of the following carburetor parts is LEAST likely to require replacement? 22.____

    A. Needle and inlet seat
    B. Fuel nozzle
    C. Cover gasket
    D. Diaphragm

23. In an air-cooled engine, poor circulation is likely to cause 23.____

    A. slow cranking
    B. poor compression
    C. valve dishing
    D. misfiring

24. Which of the following is a current rectifier that consists of a semiconducting crystal with two terminals? 24.____

A. Capacitor
B. Crank
C. Diode
D. Condenser

25. If full battery voltage reaches the starter and the fly-wheel offers normal resistance but the starter stalls under compression, which of the following is most likely to be the cause? 25.____

A. Defective field coil
B. Broken pinion
C. Loose connections in external circuit
D. Weak brush springs

---

# KEY (CORRECT ANSWERS)

1. A
2. C
3. B
4. C
5. B

6. C
7. B
8. A
9. D
10. D

11. A
12. D
13. B
14. D
15. B

16. C
17. D
18. B
19. B
20. D

21. C
22. B
23. D
24. C
25. A

---

# EXAMINATION SECTION
# TEST 1

DIRECTIONS: Each question or incomplete statement is followed by several suggested answers or completions. Select the one that BEST answers the question or completes the statement. *PRINT THE LETTER OF THE CORRECT ANSWER IN THE SPACE AT THE RIGHT.*

1. An a-c armature is ALWAYS the 1.____

   A. rotating part of the generator
   B. stationary part of the generator
   C. conductors into which voltage is induced
   D. conductors through which d-c exciter current flows

2. The armature windings of a 2-phase a-c generator are physically placed so that the induced voltages are out of phase by 2.____

   A. 30° B. 60° C. 90° D. 120°

3. When connecting a 3-phase a-c generator for delta operation, the delta closure voltage should be 3.____

   A. line voltage
   B. phase voltage
   C. approximately zero volts
   D. less than phase voltage

4. With no load on the secondary, the current in the primary is 4.____

   A. zero
   B. limited only by the resistance of the winding
   C. determined by c.e.m.f. of secondary
   D. determined by c.e.m.f. of primary

5. The a-c field is ALWAYS the 5.____

   A. rotating part of the generator
   B. stationary part of the generator
   C. conductors into which voltage is induced
   D. conductors through which d-c exciter current flows

6. The voltage induced into the armature windings is maximum when the field poles are 6.____

   A. in the neutral plane
   B. opposite the armature poles
   C. between the armature poles
   D. rotating at a high speed

7. The output frequency of an a-c generator is dependent upon the 7.____

   A. number of poles and phases
   B. rotor speed and phases

C. number of poles and the speed of the prime mover
D. number of poles and the rotor speed

8. The load rating of an a-c generator is determined by the 8.____

A. internal heat it can withstand
B. load it can carry continuously
C. load it is capable of supplying
D. overload it can carry for a specified time only

9. In a 2-phase, 3-wire a-c generator, the formula for line voltage is $E_L$ = 9.____

A. $\frac{E_P}{\cos 45^\circ}$ B. $\frac{E_P}{\tan 45^\circ}$ C. $E_P \times 0.707$ D. $E_P \times 1.73$

10. The voltage output of an a-c generator is controlled by 10.____

A. regulating the speed of the prime mover
B. varying the d-c exciter voltage
C. varying the reluctance of the air gap
D. shorting out part of the armature windings

11. The PRIMARY reason for connecting transformers wye-wye is to 11.____

A. double the input voltage
B. double the primary current
C. invert the frequency
D. decrease line losses by high voltage with low current in the line

12. The purpose of the d-c generator is to excite the 12.____

A. a-c armature
B. a-c field
C. d-c armature
D. a-c and d-c field

13. A 3-phase wye-connected a-c generator is used to produce ______ current, ______ voltage. 13.____

A. high; low
B. low; low
C. low; high
D. high; high

14. Two types of instrument transformers are 14.____

A. step-up and step-down
B. potential and high voltage
C. potential and current
D. auto and power

15. The output of a rotating field a-c generator is taken from 15.____

A. sliprings and brushes
B. commutator bars and brushes
C. fixed terminals
D. none of the above

16. Aircraft transformers are designed for 400 c.p.s. because 16.____

    A. of the 400-c.p.s. supply available in the aircraft
    B. the higher frequency permits savings of size and weight
    C. it is more stable than lower frequencies
    D. it has a higher average current flow

17. The closure voltage of a delta-connected transformer secondary is 17.____

    A. 0 volts
    B. phase voltage
    C. line voltage
    D. line voltage x 1.73

18. The revolving field type a-c generator is MOST widely used because of 18.____

    A. low armature current
    B. improved safety features
    C. low field current through fixed terminals
    D. high power from armature through sliprings

19. When using an a-c generator on a 3-phase, 4-wire system, the neutral wire 19.____

    A. maintains equal current in each phase
    B. maintains equal power in each phase
    C. maintains equal voltage in each phase
    D. has no current flow when the loads are unbalanced

20. The three principal parts of a transformer are its 20.____

    A. core, primary windings, and secondary windings
    B. primary, load, and magnetic flux
    C. primary windings, secondary windings, and magnetic flux
    D. mutual induction, magnetic flux, and windings

21. A-c generators are classified 21.____

    A. as to construction
    B. as to power output
    C. according to type of prime mover
    D. according to load connections

22. The principle of operation of a transformer is 22.____

    A. electromagnetic induction
    B. varying a conductor in a magnetic field
    C. mutual induction
    D. thermionic emission

# KEY (CORRECT ANSWERS)

1. C
2. C
3. C
4. D
5. D

6. B
7. D
8. A
9. A
10. B

11. D
12. B
13. C
14. C
15. C

16. B
17. A
18. B
19. C
20. A

21. C
22. C

---

# TEST 2

DIRECTIONS: Each question or incomplete statement is followed by several suggested answers or completions. Select the one that BEST answers the question or completes the statement. *PRINT THE LETTER OF THE CORRECT ANSWER IN THE SPACE AT THE RIGHT.*

1. The variable resistance placed in the rotor circuit of the form-wound rotor is for the purpose of ______ control. 1.____

   A. speed
   B. frequency
   C. voltage
   D. starting torque

2. The MOST common method of starting a synchronous motor is 2.____

   A. with a separate d-c motor
   B. with a cage-rotor winding
   C. manually
   D. by applying d-c to the rotor

3. Why does the capacitor motor have a higher starting torque than a split-phase motor? It has 3.____

   A. a higher power factor
   B. no displacement between start and main winding currents
   C. less displacement between start and main winding currents
   D. greater displacement between its start and main winding currents

4. The synchronous speed of an induction motor is the 4.____

   A. speed at which the rotor turns
   B. speed of the rotating field
   C. frequency of the rotor current
   D. slip in percent of rotor r.p.m.

5. Near synchronous speed, the 5.____

   A. voltage induced into the rotor is very small
   B. voltage induced into the rotor is large
   C. applied voltage on the stator is zero
   D. rotor frequency is maximum

6. What circumstances cause a lagging power factor? 6.____

   A. $I_s$ lags resultant E by $90^o$ - $I_s$ lags $E_a$ by angle $\theta$
   B. $I_s$ leads resultant E by $90^o$ - $I_s$ leads $E_a$ by angle $\theta$
   C. Resultant E lags Is by $90^o$ - $I_s$ lags $E_a$ by angle $\phi$
   D. $E_c$ leads $I_s$ by $90^o$ - $I_s$ leads $E_a$ by angle $\phi$

7. What is the direction of rotation of the shaded-pole motor in respect to the sweeping field? 7.____

   A. With the sweeping field
   B. Against the sweeping field

C. Toward the unshaded tip
D. Depends on direction motor was started

8. Increasing the number of poles in an induction motor 8.____

A. increases the field speed
B. decreases the field speed
C. decreases the motor's rated torque
D. causes the frequency of line E to drop

9. The rotor voltage is proportional to the 9.____

A. strength of the magnetic field
B. number of conductors on the stator
C. angle at which lines of force are cut
D. difference in rotor speed and the speed of the rotating field

10. The MOST common type of starter used on board ship for a-c motors is the 10.____

A. autotransformer
B. secondary capacitor
C. primary resistor
D. across-the-line

11. In the repulsion induction motor, what is the position of the brushes in relation to the stator polar axis for maximum torque? 11.____

A. $15^\circ$
B. $25^\circ$
C. $45^\circ$
D. $90^\circ$

12. Increasing the frequency of the voltage applied to an induction motor causes the 12.____

A. field speed to decrease
B. field speed to increase
C. rotor torque to decrease
D. stator current to increase

13. The purpose of the iron rotor core is to 13.____

A. decrease motor weight
B. produce eddy currents
C. reduce air gap reluctance
D. decrease permeability

14. The frequency of rotor current varies directly with the 14.____

A. applied voltage
B. resistance of the rotor
C. slip
D. number of windings on the stator

15. The efficiency of a motor is equal to the 15.____

A. torque output at synchronous speed
B. amount of current in the rotor
C. horsepower of the motor
D. ratio of its output power to its input power

16. The type of starter used when it is necessary to limit the starting current of an a-c motor is the 16.____

A. autotransformer
B. secondary resistor
C. primary resistor
D. primary capacitor

17. The type of starter used for speed control of an a-c motor is the 17.____

A. secondary resistor
B. open transition
C. closed transition
D. primary resistor

18. Motor action is BEST analyzed by applying 18.____

A. Fleming's right-hand rule
B. the magnetic laws of polarity
C. Lenz's law for self-induced voltage
D. the left-hand motor rule

19. A synchronous motor is NOT self-starting due to 19.____

A. its lack of a rotating magnetic field
B. inertia of the rotor
C. magnetic locking action between rotor and stator fields
D. its low power factor

20. The single-phase a-c motor is NOT self-starting because there is 20.____

A. inertia in the rotor
B. no high starting torque
C. no revolving magnetic field
D. a magnetic lock between the rotor and stator

21. In the a-c series motor, how are hysteresis losses minimized? By use of 21.____

A. high frequency voltage
B. laminations only
C. hard iron
D. silicon steel

22. The direction of rotation of an induction motor is 22.____

A. opposite the rotating field direction
B. same as direction of rotating field
C. determined by the number of poles
D. determined by the location of its brushes

23. A synchronous motor differs from an induction motor in that it 23.____

A. is not self-starting
B. requires an a-c and a d-c power supply
C. may be used for power factor correction
D. all of the above

24. How can the direction of rotation of a split-phase induction motor be reversed? Reverse 24.____

A. leads of main winding
B. leads of start windings
C. leads of one phase
D. any two leads

25. Fractional horsepower a-c series motors are called ______ motors. 25.____

A. induction
B. synchronous
C. universal
D. shaded-pole

---

## KEY (CORRECT ANSWERS)

1. D
2. B
3. D
4. B
5. A

6. A
7. A
8. B
9. D
10. D

11. B
12. B
13. C
14. C
15. D

16. C
17. A
18. D
19. B
20. C

21. D
22. B
23. D
24. B
25. C

---

# TEST 3

DIRECTIONS: Each question or incomplete statement is followed by several suggested answers or completions. Select the one that BEST answers the question or completes the statement. *PRINT THE LETTER OF THE CORRECT ANSWER IN THE SPACE AT THE RIGHT.*

1. A d-c generator is a rotating machine that converts ______ energy. 1.____

   A. electrical energy to mechanical
   B. mechanical energy to electrical
   C. low mechanical energy to a higher level of mechanical
   D. low electrical energy to a higher level of electrical

2. Commutator segments are insulated from each other by 2.____

   A. small strips of wood
   B. a rubber insert
   C. laminated varnish
   D. sheet mica

3. The brushes that carry the current from the commutator to the external circuit are made of 3.____

   A. carbon and lead
   B. carbon and graphite
   C. graphite and lead
   D. graphite and zinc

4. The heat-radiating ability of very small armature conductors, as compared to large armature conductors, is 4.____

   A. the same
   B. higher
   C. lower
   D. there is no relation

5. The degree that the neutral plane of a generator will shift under load is ______ the load. 5.____

   A. inversely proportional to
   B. proportional to
   C. always less than proportional to
   D. independent of

6. D-c generators are classified according to the manner in which 6.____

   A. they are used
   B. the field windings are connected to the load
   C. the armature circuit is connected to the load
   D. the field windings are connected to the armature circuit

7. The ONLY type of compound generator commonly used is the 7.____

   A. over compounded
   B. flat compounded
   C. stabilized shunt
   D. cumulative compounded

8. On one end of the tilted plate regulator, the graphite plates are separated by mica spacers, while on the other end they are separated by 8.____

   A. platinum contacts
   B. silver contacts
   C. zinc contacts
   D. a carbon shoe

9. In the rocking disk regulator, when the terminal voltage of the generator starts to fall, the disk movement 9.____

   A. opens the circuit to the solenoid
   B. short-circuits more of the resistors
   C. short-circuits less of the resistors
   D. completes the circuit to the solenoid

10. The 3-wire generator is similar to the 2-wire generator except that the armature winding is tapped at ______ degrees. 10.____

   A. 30 mechanical
   B. 90 electrical
   C. 180 electrical
   D. 30 electrical

11. The name given to the mechanical power source used to turn the armature of a d-c generator is the 11.____

   A. motor driver
   B. machine driver
   C. prime mover
   D. rotor

12. Flashover between the commutator segments in a high-voltage d-c generator is prevented by 12.____

   A. reducing the number of segments
   B. increasing the number of segments
   C. reducing the number of field coils
   D. increasing the number of field coils

13. The distance between the two sides of a coil in a d-c generator armature is called 13.____

   A. coil pitch
   B. commutator pitch
   C. pole span
   D. pole pitch

14. The effects of armature reaction in a generator are reduced by the use of 14.____

   A. commutating windings
   B. interpoles
   C. commutating windings and interpoles
   D. compensating windings and commutating poles

15. The need for shifting the brushes of a d-c generator as its load changes has been eliminated by the use of 15.____

   A. interpoles
   B. commutating poles
   C. compensating windings
   D. larger brushes

16. A shunt generator will build up to full terminal voltage with no external load connected to it due to 16.____

   A. the large conductors used in the armature
   B. motor action of the generator
   C. interpoles
   D. self-excitation

17. The percent regulation of a generator having a no-load e.m.f. of 220 volts and a full-load e.m.f. of 215 volts is APPROXIMATELY 17.____

A. 3% B. 45% C. 0.02% D. 2%

18. The purpose of the vibrator-type current limiter is to automatically limit the output current of the generator to its 18.____

A. preset value
B. minimum rated value
C. maximum rated value
D. saturation point

19. The main differences between shipboard d-c generators and aircraft d-c generators are 19.____

A. size, rating, and appearance
B. size, appearance, and function
C. size and rating only
D. appearance, rating, and function

20. The part of a d-c generator into which the working voltage is induced is the 20.____

A. yoke
B. field poles
C. armature
D. commutator

21. Power lost in heat in the windings due to the flow of current through the copper is known as 21.____

A. eddy current loss
B. hysteresis loss
C. copper loss
D. none is correct

22. Compensating windings are imbedded in the pole faces parallel to the armature conductors and are electrically connected with the armature windings in 22.____

A. parallel
B. series-parallel
C. series
D. numbers equal to the number of armature conductors

23. As armature current of a generator increases, motor reaction force 23.____

A. decreases
B. remains the same
C. increases
D. has no relation to armature current

24. The small variable shunt connected across the series field coils, to permit adjustment of the degree of compounding, is a 24.____

A. diverter B. divider C. resistor D. rheostat

25. The MAJOR difference between various voltage regulator systems is merely the method by which ______ controlled. 25.____

A. field circuit resistance and current are
B. armature circuit resistance is
C. load circuit resistance is
D. armature current and load resistance are

# KEY (CORRECT ANSWERS)

1. B
2. D
3. B
4. B
5. B
6. D
7. C
8. B
9. B
10. C
11. C
12. B
13. A
14. D
15. A
16. D
17. D
18. C
19. A
20. C
21. C
22. C
23. C
24. A
25. A

---

# TEST 4

DIRECTIONS: Each question or incomplete statement is followed by several suggested answers or completions. Select the one that BEST answers the question or completes the statement. *PRINT THE LETTER OF THE CORRECT ANSWER IN THE SPACE AT THE RIGHT.*

1. The MOST convenient method of determining the direction of induced motion of a current-carrying conductor in a magnetic field is by 1.____

   A. applying the right-hand rule for motors
   B. applying the left-hand rule for motors
   C. using a small permanent magnet
   D. observation of the location of the conductor

2. The formula for torque developed by a motor is T = 2.____

   A. $\frac{K_t}{\phi I_a}$  B. $K_t^2 \phi I_a$  C. $K_t \phi I_a^2$  D. $K_t \phi I_a$

3. The effective voltage ($E_{eff}$) drop in a motor's armature is determined by $E_{eff}$ = 3.____

   A. $E_{app}$ + c.e.m.f.  B. $E_{app}$ x c.e.m.f.
   C. $E_{app}$ - c.e.m.f.  D. $\frac{\text{c.e.m.f.}}{E_{app}}$

4. Which of the following is TRUE regarding the speed regulation of a shunt motor? It has a ______ speed characteristic under ______ loads. 4.____

   A. constant; varying  B. varying; varying
   C. varying; constant  D. none of the above

5. The PRIMARY advantage of the differentially compounded motor is that it(s) 5.____

   A. is stable under heavy loads
   B. speed regulation is very good if load is not excessive
   C. has good speed regulation under varying loads
   D. will start under a heavy load

6. If the no-load speed of a shunt motor is 1,800 r.p.m. and the full-load speed is 1,475 r.p.m., the speed regulation is 6.____

   A. 18%  B. 22%  C. 2.2%  D. 1.8%

7. The input power of a series motor is the product of the applied voltage and 7.____

   A. counter e.m.f.
   B. torque
   C. current through the armature and the field
   D. current through the armature and counter e.m.f.

8. The disadvantage of the time-element automatic starter is that the 8.____

   A. cost is high
   B. wiring is complicated
   C. construction is too heavy to be practical
   D. motor is not protected on overload

9. The starting resistor of the shunt current-limit starter is connected in _______ with the _______. 9.____

   A. parallel; motor armature
   B. series; accelerating conductor
   C. series; field winding of the motor
   D. series; armature of the motor

10. A motor which has an output of 820 watts and an input of 960 watts has an efficiency of APPROXIMATELY 10.____

   A. 90% B. 85% C. 75% D. 70%

11. The horsepower developed by a motor depends MAINLY upon which of the following two factors? 11.____

   A. Speed and voltage
   B. Speed and torque
   C. Torque and voltage
   D. Torque and watts

12. A series motor is more adaptable where a 12.____

   A. small variation of torque and speed is needed
   B. wide variation of torque but a small variation of speed is needed
   C. wide variation of torque is required, and wide variations in speed are allowable
   D. constant speed is needed

13. Cumulative compound motors are BEST suited for use where 13.____

   A. small starting torque is required
   B. small changes in speed can be tolerated
   C. the load may be removed from the motor with safety
   D. constant speed under varying load is required

14. What is the output power in watts of a shunt motor of 1 horsepower operating on 100 volts at 910 r.p.m., armature current of 9 amps, and a line current of 10 amps? _______ watts. 14.____

   A. 98.4 B. 472 C. 646 D. 815

15. The counter e.m.f. of a motor is zero when the 15.____

   A. motor is at rated speed
   B. armature is not turning
   C. motor is almost up to rated speed
   D. armature has just begun to turn

16. The operation of the c.e.m.f. starter depends upon the 16.____

A. size of the orifice in the dashpot
B. c.e.m.f. developed across the armature
C. accelerating contacts
D. interlocking relays

17. In a shunt current-limit starter, the number of starting resistors that are commonly used is 17.____

A. one
B. two or three
C. five or six
D. more than ten

18. The speed of a motor with no load, with an increase of resistance in series with the field winding, will 18.____

A. not be affected
B. decrease
C. increase
D. fluctuate rapidly

19. The generated voltage (c.e.m.f.) of a motor 19.____

A. opposes the impressed (source) voltage
B. opposes any change in load
C. aids the impressed (source) voltage
D. none of the above

20. When a load is applied to a shunt motor, which one of the following will happen? Speed ______, c.e.m.f. goes ______. 20.____

A. decreases; up
B. increases; down
C. increases; up
D. decreases; down

21. On a time-element starter, what determines the speed with which the resistance is cut out? 21.____

A. Size of the orifice in the dashpot
B. Counter e.m.f. of the armature
C. Interlocking relays
D. Accelerating contacts

22. The coil of the accelerating contactor of the shunt current-limit starter is caused to become energized by which of the following when the motor speeds up? 22.____

A. Series relay contacts closing
B. Series relay contacts opening
C. The no-voltage release
D. Holding relay contacts

23. In the series current-limit starter, the flux is prevented from closing the contactor before it has time to lock open by 23.____

A. an open coil
B. the spring tension of the contacts
C. the starting resistor
D. a short-circuited coil

24. The d-c motor armature whose speed is to be controlled by the Ward-Leonard system is fed by a 24.____

    A. 3-phase motor
    B. d-c supply in parallel with a rheostat
    C. d-c generator
    D. rectifier

25. In the rocking disk regulator, when the terminal voltage of the generator starts to fall, the solenoid is weakened and the weight rocks the disk 25.____

    A. upward
    B. to the left
    C. to the right
    D. downward

---

# KEY (CORRECT ANSWERS)

1. A
2. D
3. C
4. A
5. B

6. B
7. C
8. D
9. D
10. B

11. B
12. C
13. C
14. D
15. B

16. B
17. B
18. C
19. A
20. D

21. A
22. A
23. D
24. C
25. D

---

# TEST 5

DIRECTIONS: Each question or incomplete statement is followed by several suggested answers or completions. Select the one that BEST answers the question or completes the statement. *PRINT THE LETTER OF THE CORRECT ANSWER IN THE SPACE AT THE RIGHT.*

1. A wattmeter is connected in a circuit with the current coil _______ with the load. 1.____

   A. and the potential coil in parallel
   B. in parallel and the potential coil in series
   C. in series and the potential coil in parallel
   D. and the potential coil in series

2. A metallic rectifier is a device that 2.____

   A. converts d.c. to a.c.
   B. offers high opposition to current in two directions
   C. is classed as a unidirectional conductor
   D. has two good conductors of electricity

3. The amperage rating of the secondary windings of a current transformer is rated at _______ amps. 3.____

   A. 400 B. 12 C. 5 D. 2,000

4. In the iron-vane power factor meter, the vanes are magnetized by current flowing in 4.____

   A. coil A
   B. coil B
   C. coil C
   D. all three coils simultaneously

5. In a wattmeter, if the voltage or current safe rating is exceeded, the meter 5.____

   A. reading may not indicate overload
   B. will peg to the right of the scale
   C. will not be affected
   D. will not indicate power factor

6. The path for current flow through a rectifier cell is 6.____

   A. from the conductor, across the barrier layer, through the semiconductor
   B. from the semiconductor, across to the barrier layer, through the conductor
   C. in the direction of the arrow
   D. through the fin assembly

7. In a capacitor bridge, to find the value of an unknown capacitor, what is used to bring the circuit into balance? 7.____

   A. Two variable capacitors
   B. Capacitive reactance of capacitors
   C. Two resistors
   D. Two potentiometers

8. A watt-hour meter reads the product as 8.____

A. energy and time
B. power and current
C. power and time
D. power and energy

9. Under normal conditions, the fin assembly in a rectifier is used to 9.____

A. apply uniform pressure to reduce internal resistance
B. carry current
C. create resistance
D. dissipate excess heat

10. When using the vibrating-reed frequency meter, if the frequency of the current is 112 cycles, the reed will be marked ______ c.p.s. 10.____

A. 55
B. 56
C. 60
D. 112

11. In the iron-vane power factor meter, the spiral springs 11.____

A. are eliminated
B. return the pointer to zero
C. oppose torque
D. carry current to coils A and B

12. Instruments for measuring high voltage circuits become inaccurate when connected directly to high voltage because of 12.____

A. electrostatic forces acting on the transformer
B. inexpensiveness of instrument indicators
C. high hysteresis effect on indicating element
D. electrostatic forces acting on indicating element

13. The normal efficiency of a copper-oxide rectifier is from 13.____

A. 25% to 55%
B. 55% to 65%
C. 85% to 100%
D. 65% to 85%

14. In the moving-disk frequency meter, the magnetic field tends to produce rotation toward 14.____

A. coil A
B. the magnetizing coil
C. the shorted coil
D. coil B

15. When reading a watt-hour meter, the dials are read 15.____

A. from the next highest number that the needle has just passed
B. left to right
C. right to left
D. and subtracted

16. Instruments that are used to measure voltage and current regardless of circuit ratings are 16.____

A. instrument transformers
B. autotransformers
C. electrodynamometers
D. D'Arsonvals

17. A D'Arsonval d-c type instrument can be converted to read a.c. by using 17.____

A. a bridge rectifier unit
B. four rectifier cells connected in series
C. a selenium rectifier
D. a copper-oxide rectifier

18. In the moving-disk frequency meter, the current through coil B varies 18.____

A. inversely with the frequency
B. directly with the frequency
C. because it is connected in parallel
D. because inductive reactance is constant

19. A safety precaution to follow when using a potential transformer is to 19.____

A. ground the secondary
B. ground the primary
C. insulate for high current
D. connect it in series with the line

20. The primary of a current transformer is always connected in 20.____

A. series with the primary
B. series with the line
C. parallel with the line
D. parallel with the power source

21. The wattmeter is a(n) 21.____

A. D'Arsonval meter
B. electrodynamometer
C. potential coil meter
D. iron-vane meter

22. A power factor meter measures the 22.____

A. phase angle between current and voltage
B. sine of the phase angle between current and voltage
C. ratio of apparent power to true power
D. ratio of true power to apparent power

23. The secondary of a current transformer should NOT be open-circuited because 23.____

A. of high current in the primary
B. of high voltage in the secondary
C. of low current in the primary
D. it is not grounded

24. In the crossed-coil power factor meter, circuit continuity to the coils is provided by 24.____

A. stationary current coil
B. the resistor
C. the inductor
D. three spiral springs

25. In the carbon-pile type regulator, the mechanical pressure on the carbon pile is applied by the 25.____

A. wafer spring
B. potential coil
C. iron core of the potential coil
D. rheostat

---

# KEY (CORRECT ANSWERS)

1. C
2. C
3. C
4. C
5. A

6. A
7. D
8. C
9. D
10. B

11. A
12. D
13. D
14. C
15. C

16. A
17. A
18. A
19. A
20. B

21. B
22. D
23. B
24. D
25. A

---

# ELECTRICITY
# EXAMINATION SECTION
# TEST 1

DIRECTIONS: Each question or incomplete statement is followed by several suggested answers or completions. Select the one that BEST answers the question or completes the statement. *PRINT THE LETTER OF THE CORRECT ANSWER IN THE SPACE AT THE RIGHT.*

1. A unit of inductance is the 1._____
   A. microfarad B. milliohm C. millihenry D. micromho

2. The resistance which is equivalent to 10 megohms is 2._____
   A. $1 \times 10^8$ ohms B. $1 \times 10^7$ ohms
   C. $1 \times 10^6$ ohms D. $1 \times 10^5$ ohms

3. A two-microfarad capacitor is connected in parallel with an eight-microfarad capacitor. The TOTAL capacitance of this combination is 3._____
   A. 0.25 microfarad B. 0.5 microfarad
   C. 1.6 microfarads D. 10 microfarads

4. A current of 10 milliamperes is 4._____
   A. 0.0001 amperes B. 0.001 amperes
   C. 0.01 amperes D. 0.1 amperes

5. If 120 volts are impressed across a resistance of 300 ohms, 5. the power dissipated by the resistance is 5._____
   A. 0.4 watt B. 2.5 watts C. 36 watts D. 48 watts

6. The number of circular mils in a conductor 0.04 inch in diameter is 6._____
   A. 1600 circular mils B. 1260 circular mils
   C. 126 circular mils D. 40 circular mils

7. When an electrical device is connected across a 208-volt, 60-Hertz, A.C. supply, the peak voltage across the device is, most nearly, 7._____
   A. 208 volts B. 295 volts C. 360 volts D. 416 volts

8. The colors of the three conductors in a 3-conductor cable DS for a 120/208-volt system should be 8._____
   A. white, black and green B. white, red and blue
   C. white, blue and black D. white, black and red

9. A 15-ohm resistor is connected in parallel with a 10-ohm resistor. This combination of resistors are in turn connected in series with a 4-ohm resistor. The TOTAL resistance of this combination of three resistors is 9._____
   A. 29.0 ohms B. 10.0 ohms C. 6.0 ohms D. 4.2 ohms

10. The insulation resistance of a certain conductor is 16 megohms. If the conductor is cut into two equal lengths, the insulation resistance of each length is 10._____
    A. 32 megohms B. 16 megohms C. 8 megohms D. 4 megohms

11. A certain circuit consists of a reactance with a value of 18 ohms at 60 Hertz connected in series with a 6-ohm resistance. When this circuit is connected to a 120-volt, 60-Hertz, A.C. supply, the current in the circuit is 11._____
   A. 20 amperes B. 15 amperes C. 12 amperes D. 10 amperes

12. A resistance of 2.5 ohms is connected across the terminals of a battery which has an open circuit voltage of 12 volts and an internal resistance of 0.5 ohms. The current in this circuit is, most nearly, 12._____
   A. 4.0 amperes B. 4.8 amperes C. 6.0 amperes D. 24 amperes

13. Assuming that the resistance of a No. 10 (AWG) conductor at 68°F is approximately 1 ohm per 1000 ft., the resistance of 1000 ft., of a No. 13 (AWG) conductor at 68°F is, approximately, 13._____
   A. 0.5 ohm B. 1.26 ohms C. 2.0 ohms D. 3.0 ohms

14. Suppose that the line voltage of a 3-phase circuit is E, the line current, in amperes, is I and the power factor is P.F. The formula for the power consumed, in watts, in this circuit is 14._____
   A. $\sqrt{3}$ EI P.F. B. EI P.F. C. 3 EI P.F. D. $\sqrt{2}$ EI P.F.

15. Assume that a current density of 1000 amperes per square inch is allowable for bus bars. A certain bus bar which has a circular cross section is 1.5 inches in diameter and is 3 feet long. The MAXIMUM allowable current for this bus bar is, most nearly, 15._____
   A. 400 amperes B. 1500 amperes
   C. 1800 amperes D. 7200 amperes

16. The color of the label on a 600-volt fuse should be. 16._____
   A. blue B. green C. red D. yellow

17. Of the following, the colors of the three conductors of a 3-conductor cable for a 277/490-volt system used to supply 277-volt fluorescent lights should be 17._____
   A. white, brown, and yellow B. white, black, and yellow
   C. white, red, and orange D. white, blue, and orange

18. Although all fuses on a panel are good, the clips on the fuse in circuit No. 1 are much hotter than the clips of the other fuses. The most likely cause of this condition is that 18._____
   A. circuit No. 1 is greatly over-loaded
   B. circuit No. 1 is carrying much less than rated load
   C. the fuse of circuit No. 1 is very loose in its clips
   D. the room temperature is abnormally high

19. Of the following colors, the one that may be used for the 19. ground wire for a piece of portable equipment is 19._____
   A. gray B. green C. white D. black

20. Fixture wire should NOT be smaller than 20._____
   A. No. 14 B. No. 16 C. No. 18 D. No. 20

---

# KEY (CORRECT ANSWERS)

1. C
2. B
3. D
4. C
5. D
6. A
7. B
8. D
9. B
10. A
11. C
12. A
13. C
14. A
15. C
16. C
17. A
18. C
19. B
20. C

---

# TEST 2

DIRECTIONS: Each question or incomplete statement is followed by several suggested answers or completions. Select the one that BEST answers the question or completes the statement. *PRINT THE LETTER OF THE CORRECT ANSWER IN THE SPACE AT THE RIGHT.*

1. An example of an adjustable wrench is the 1.______
   A. Bristol wrench
   B. Crescent wrench
   C. Allen wrench
   D. box wrench

2. The term which is defined by the electrical code as a set of conductors originating at a distribution center other than the main distribution center, and supplying one or more branch circuit distribution centers, is a 2.______
   A. raceway
   B. main
   C. sub-feeder
   D. service

3. When three No. 10-type R wires are run in the same conduit, 3. the allowable current-carrying capacity of each wire is 3.______
   A. 15 amperes
   B. 20 amperes
   C. 25 amperes
   D. 30 amperes

4. Two No. 12-type R conductors in a 3/4-inch conduit are carrying the maximum allowable current to an appliance. It is desired to double the load. Of the following, the BEST way to supply this new load is to 4.______
   A. run two more No. 12-type R conductors in multiple with the existing conductors
   B. remove the existing conductors and run two No. 10-type R conductors in the conduit
   C. replace the existing conduit and conductors with a 1-inch conduit and two No. 10-type R conductors
   D. remove the existing conductors and run two No. 8-type R conductors in the conduit

5. According to the electrical code, No. 1/0 copper conductors in vertical raceways should be supported at intervals of not greater than 5.______
   A. 100 feet
   B. 80 feet
   C. 60 feet
   D. 50 feet

6. A universal motor is also a 6.______
   A. squirrel-cage motor
   B. synchronous motor
   C. series motor
   D. wound-rotor motor

7. In a run of non-metallic conduit between two outlets, the MAXIMUM number of equivalent quarter bends permitted is 7.______
   A. 2
   B. 3
   C. 4
   D. 5

8. The MINIMUM number of wattmeters required to measure the power in an unbalanced 3-phase, 4-wire system, is 8.______
   A. 1
   B. 2
   C. 3
   D. 4

9. An A.C. ammeter which reads 5 amperes full scale and a voltmeter which reads 150 volts full scale are properly connected, without instrument transformers, to various loads on a 120-volt A.C. circuit. The MAXIMUM load that can be safely measured under these conditions is 9.______
   A. 750 watts at 80% leading power factor
   B. 750 watts at unity power factor
   C. 600 watts at 80% lagging power factor
   D. 600 watts at unity power factor

10. In a single-phase A.C. circuit, the voltage is E, the current is I, the resistance is R, and the wattage is W. A formula which will give the power factor of the circuit is: 10.______
   A. E I ÷ RB.  B. $I^2 \div R$  C. W ÷ E I  D. E I ÷ W

11. A single-phase 100-ampere load is fed from a 120-volt panel board 500 feet away by means of two conductors. Each conductor has a resistivity of 10.5 ohms per circular-mil-foot. The size of conductor that will cause the voltage drop to the load to be most nearly 2 ½ %, is 11.______
   A. 148,000 C M  B. 175,000 C M
   C. 350,000 C M  D. 420,000 C M

12. The method of motor control which is called jogging is the 12.______
   A. quick reversal of the direction of rotation of a motor
   B. repeated closing of the circuit to start a motor from rest in order to get a small movement
   C. using up of the energy in a motor by making it act as a generator with a resistive load
   D. slowing of a motor by using it as a generator to return energy to the power supply system

13. When the armature current drawn by a certain D.C. series motor is 10 amperes-, the torque is 10 pound-feet. If the current is increased to 20 amperes, the torque is 13.______
   A. 5 pound-feet  B. 15 pound-feet
   C. 20 pound-feet  D. 40 pound-feet

14. The proper way to reverse the direction of rotation of a repulsion motor is to 14.______
   A. reverse the connections to the auxiliary field winding
   B. move the brushes to the opposite side of the pole axis
   C. interchange the line leads
   D. interchange the main field connections

15. A D.C. series motor is running at rated load and rated speed. If the entire load is suddenly removed, the 15.______
   A. field strength will increase
   B. armature current will increase
   C. efficiency will increase
   D. motor will start to "race"

16. One way of distinguishing an A.C. series motor from aD.C. series motor of the same horsepower and voltage rating is that the A.C. motor has 16.______
   A. relatively fewer poles
   B. a larger armature
   C. more turns of the same size wire in the field
   D. fewer turns of the same size wire in the armature

17. The proper way to reverse the direction of rotation of a cumulative compound motor without changing its operating characteristics is to 17.______
   A. interchange the connections to the armature
   B. reverse the polarity of the supply
   C. interchange the connections to the shunt field
   D. interchange the connections to the series field

18. A certain ideal transformer has a primary voltage of 2200 volts and a secondary voltage of 110 volts. The primary-to-secondary-turns ratio of this transformer is 18.____
   A. 22 to 1 B. 20 to 1 C. 1 to 11 D. 1 to 20

19. A light is to be controlled independently from six separate locations. Of the following, the group of switches required to do this is 19.____
   A. two 3-way, two S.P.S.T. and two 4-way
   B. three 3-way and three 4-way
   C. four 3-way and two 4-way
   D. two 3-way and four 4-way

20. A D.C. motor operating at 110 volts and drawing 40 amperes has an efficiency of 80%. The horsepower output of this motor is, most nearly, 20.____
   A. 1 B. 3 C. 5 D. 7

---

# KEY (CORRECT ANSWERS)

| | |
|---|---|
| 1. B | 11. C |
| 2. C | 12. B |
| 3. D | 13. D |
| 4. D | 14. B |
| 5. A | 15. D |
| 6. C | 16. B |
| 7. C | 17. A |
| 8. C | 18. B |
| 9. D | 19. D |
| 10. C | 20. C |

---

# TEST 3

DIRECTIONS: Each question or incomplete statement is followed by several suggested answers or completions. Select the one that BEST answers the question or completes the statement. *PRINT THE LETTER OF THE CORRECT ANSWER IN THE SPACE AT THE RIGHT.*

1. The instrument which should be used to measure the insulation resistance of a motor is a (n) 1.______
   A. ohmmeter B. megger
   C. ammeter D. varmeter

2. Of the following, the piece of equipment which should be used to locate a shorted coil in the armature of a D.C. motor is a 2.______
   A. permeameter B. varley loop growler
   C. fluxmeter D. growler

3. Braking a motor by reversing the line polarity is called 3.______
   A. plugging B. resistance braking
   C. inching D. regenerative braking

4. The full load-speed of a 120-volt, 60-Hertz, four-pole squirrel cage motor, which has a slip of 6% at full load, is, most nearly, 4.______
   A. 1600 rpm B. 1700 rpm C. 1800 rpm D. rpm

5. The formula for the resistance of one branch of a delta which is equivalent to a given wye is $RAB = \frac{ab+bc+ca}{c}$ If a = b = c = 2 ohms, the value of RAB is, most nearly, 5.______
   A. 3 ohms B. 6 ohms C. 9 ohms D. 12 ohms

6. A 3-phase wound-rotor induction motor is running hot and is slower than usual for the load. When stopped, the motor hums and fails to start up again. A possible cause of this condition is that 6.______
   A. the resistance in the rheostat is too low
   B. the brush tension is too great
   C. one phase of the stator is open
   D. the frequency of the supply is too high

7. A 208-volt, 3-phase, A.C. supply is connected to the stator of a motor. D.C. is supplied to its rotor by a small generator directly connected to the end of the motor's shaft. Of the following, it is most likely that this motor is a 7.______
   A. squirrel-cage motor B. wound-rotor motor
   C. repulsion motor D. synchronous motor

8. Assume that two single-phase wattmeters are properly connected to measure the power consumed by a 3-phase, 3-wire system. The wattmeters read 1000 watts and 0 watts, respectively. The power factor of the system is 8.______
   A. 0 B. 0.5 C. 0.8 D. 1.0

9. The range of a D.C. ammeter is most often increased by the use of a 9.______
   A. multiplier B. current transformer
   C. shunt D. potential transformer

10. According to the electrical code, three-way and four-way switches should be classed as 10._____
   A. D.P. D.T. switches
   B. single-pole switches
   C. D.P. S.T. switches
   D. three-pole switches

11. The definition of a trip-free circuit breaker is one that is designed 11._____
   A. for remote control from any desired location
   B. to be free from damage by "chattering" of the contacts
   C. to be free from damage of the contacts by arcing
   D. so that it will open even if the handle is manually held down

12. Of the following, the BEST hacksaw blade to use to cut EMT is one having 12._____
   A. 32 teeth per inch
   B. 14 teeth per inch
   C. 12 teeth per inch
   D. 10 teeth per inch

13. The one of the following fasteners that is BEST to use to secure an outlet box to a brick wall is 13._____
   A. toggle bolts
   B. lead expansion anchors
   C. wooden plugs
   D. steel masonry nails

14. Of the following, the usual way of extending the range of an A.C. ammeter is to use a 14._____
   A. straight shunt
   B. series resistance
   C. current transformer
   D. diode

15. In variable-speed induction motors, the phases should be connected in 15._____
   A. series delta for high speed and parallel star for low speed in constant torque motors
   B. parallel star for high speed and series delta for low speed in constant torque motors
   C. parallel star for high speed and series delta for low speed in constant horsepower motors
   D. series star for high speed and parallel star for low speed in constant horsepower motors

16. Of the following, the type of fire extinguisher which is suitable for use on fires in or near electrical equipment is the 16._____
   A. soda-acid fire extinguisher
   B. stored pressure water fire extinguisher
   C. foam fire extinguisher
   D. carbon dioxide fire extinguisher

17. A portable drill is marked with the symbol ⧈. This means that it 17._____
   A. should be used for high voltage circuits
   B. can properly operate at 25-Hertz A.C.
   C. has double insulation
   D. is a D.C. drill

18. Conductors with lead sheaths are run in a 1-inch nonmetallic conduit. The code requires that the minimum radius of the curve to the inner edge of a field bend of this conduit should be 18._____
   A. 6 inches
   B. 11 inches
   C. 16 inches
   D. 21 inches

19. The minimum permissible radius of the curve of the inner edge of any bend in armored cable is the diameter of the cable. 19.____
    A. four times
    B. five times
    C. six times
    D. eight times

20. Connectors of the "visible type" (i.e., having peep holes) are required when making connections between outlet boxes and 20.____
    A. flexible conduit
    B. electric metallic tubing
    C. armored cable
    D. rigid iron conduit

---

# KEY (CORRECT ANSWERS)

| | |
|---|---|
| 1. B | 11. D |
| 2. D | 12. A |
| 3. A | 13. B |
| 4. B | 14. C |
| 5. B | 15. B |
| 6. C | 16. D |
| 7. D | 17. C |
| 8. B | 18. B |
| 9. C | 19. B |
| 10. B | 20. C |

---

# TEST 4

DIRECTIONS: Each question or incomplete statement is followed by several suggested answers or completions. Select the one that BEST answers the question or completes the statement. *PRINT THE LETTER OF THE CORRECT ANSWER IN THE SPACE AT THE RIGHT.*

1. The MAXIMUM spacing permitted between the supports of 1-inch rigid nonmetallic Conduit containing RHH wire is 1._____
   A. 2 1/2 feet B. 3 1/2 feet
   C. 4 feet D. 5 feet

2. The MINIMUM permitted size of flexible metal conduit containing leads to recessed light fixtures is 2._____
   A. 1/4 inch B. 3/8 inch
   C. 1/2 inch D. 5/8 inch

3. A 16-foot extension ladder is to be placed against a vertical wall. According to most safety manuals, the distance between the foot of the ladder and the base of the wall should be 3._____
   A. less than 1' 0"
   B. exactly l' 6"
   C. 1/12 the length of the ladder
   D, 1/4 the length of the ladder

4. The MAXIMUM voltage defined as low potential is 4._____
A. 208 volts B. 477 volts C. 600 volts D. 1100 volts

5. In which one of the following locations are types NM and NMC cables permitted? 5._____
   A. Hoistways B. Battery rooms
   C. Unfinished basements D. Commercial garages

6. A bank of three single-phase transformers, each having a ratio of 20 to 1, are connected with their primaries in delta and their secondaries in wye. If the low-voltage windings are used as the secondaries, and the line voltage on the secondary side is 480 volts, the line voltage on the primary side is 6._____
   A. 3,200 volts B. 5,540 volts
   C. 9,600 volts D. 16,600 volts

7. Of the following tools, the proper one to use to make a hole in a brick wall is a 7._____
   A. carbon steel drill B. cold chisel
   C. diamond point chisel D. star drill

8. A light-and-power circuit consists of four wires colored white, black, blue and red, respectively. In order to properly de-energize this circuit, it is necessary to install a switch which simultaneously opens the 8._____
   A. blue, black, and white wires
   B. black, red, and white wires
   C. red, black, and blue wires
   D. red, white, and blue wires

9. A heavy object should be lifted by first crouching and firmly grasping the object to be lifted. Then, the worker should lift 9.______
   A. using his back muscles and keeping his legs bent
   B. by straightening his legs and keeping his back as straight as possible
   C. using his arm muscles and keeping his back nearly horizontal
   D. using his arm muscles and keeping his feet close together

10. When mouth-to-mouth resuscitation is administered to an adult, the recommended breathing-rate of the rescuer is 10.______
    A. 4 breaths per minute
    B. 12 breaths per minute
    C. 25 breaths per minute
    D. 35 breaths per minute

11. The standard number of threads per inch on 1-inch rigid-steel conduit is 11.______
    A. 16 threads per inch
    B. 14 threads per inch
    C. 11 1/2 threads per inch
    D. 8 threads per inch

12. An example of type S fuse is a 12.______
    A. standard ferrule contact cartridge fuse of the renewable type
    B. standard knife-blade contact one-time fuse
    C. dual element time-delay type of standard screw base plug fuse
    D. tamper-resistant type of time-delay plug fuse

13. The method of wiring known as concealed knob-and-tube work 13.______
    A. should not be used in the hollow spaces of walls and ceilings of any building
    B. may be used in the hollow spaces of walls and ceilings of residences
    C. Test 4/KEYS
    D. may be used in the hollow spaces of walls and ceilings of commercial garages
    E. should not be used in the hollow spaces of walls and ceilings of offices

14. The one of the following which is BEST to use to keep a commutator smooth is 14.______
    A. No. 1/0 emery cloth
    B. No. 00 sandpaper
    C. No. 2 steel wool
    D. a wire brush

15. A photoelectric relay used in conjunction with the controls for boiler room equipment uses a pentode amplifier. 15.______
    The one of the following elements of the pentode which receives the signal is the
    A. plate
    B. screen grid
    C. control grid
    D. suppressor grid

16. A pair of wires which can be run in multiple is one 16.______
    A. No. 2 type R and one No. 1 type R, each 100 ft. long
    B. one No. 1/0 type R and one No. 1/0 type AA, each 100 ft. long
    C. two No. 2 type AA, each 200 ft. long
    D. two No. 1/0 type R, each 100 ft. long

17. Knobs used in knob-and-tube work are usually made of 17._____
    A. molded asbestos
    B. wood
    C. porcelain
    D. steatite

18. As the speed of a fractional-horsepower, split-phase, single-phase, induction motor of the capacitor-start, induction-run type, increases and approaches full-load speed, the auxiliary winding circuit is 18._____
    A. closed by a thermal switch
    B. opened by a thermal switch
    C. closed by a centrifugal switch
    D. opened by a centrifugal switch

19. The SMALLEST size of wire which is required to have stranded conductors is 19._____
    A. No. 10 B. No. 8 C. No. 6 D. No. 4

20. The MAIN purpose of the electrical code is 20._____
    A. economy B. neatness C. efficiency D. safety

---

## KEY (CORRECT ANSWERS)

|  |  |
|---|---|
| 1. A | 11. C |
| 2. B | 12. D |
| 3. D | 13. B |
| 4. C | 14. B |
| 5. C | 15. C |
| 6. B | 16. D |
| 7. D | 17. C |
| 8. C | 18. D |
| 9. B | 19. C |
| 10. B | 20. D |

---

# EXAMINATION SECTION
# TEST 1

DIRECTIONS: Each question or incomplete statement is followed by several suggested answers or completions. Select the one that BEST answers the question or completes the statement. *PRINT THE LETTEE OF THE CORRECT ANSWER IN THE SPACE AT THE RIGHT.*

1. An AC circuit consists only of a pure inductance and a power source. The relationship between the voltage and the current in this circuit is that the 1.____

   A. voltage lags the current
   B. current leads the voltage
   C. current lags the voltage
   D. voltage and current are in phase

2. The power factor of a load is equal to the ______ power divided by the ______ power. 2.____

   A. apparent; true
   B. true; apparent
   C. reactive; apparent
   D. apparent; reactive

3. A 10-ohm and a 20-ohm resistor are connected in parallel. The total line current drawn by this parallel combination is 30 amps. Under these conditions, the line voltage will be ______ volts. 3.____

   A. 150  B. 200  C. 300  D. 600

4. A 20-ohm resistor is connected in series with a parallel combination of two resistors, one of which is 10 ohms, the other 40 ohms. If the voltage across the parallel combination is 40 volts, the voltage across the 20-ohm series resistor is ______ volts. 4.____

   A. 20  B. 40  C. 80  D. 100

5. A certain 120-volt single-phase AC circuit has a power factor of 80 percent and a watt-meter reading of 1150 watts. The current drawn by the circuit is ______ amperes. 5.____

   A. 8  B. 10  C. 12  D. 14

6. If the voltage between lines of a 3-phase, 3-wire delta connected system is 2400 volts, then the phase voltage is ______ volts. 6.____

   A. 2400  B. 2080  C. 1380  D. 1200

7. A circuit consists of an inductive reactance of 15 ohms and a resistor of 20 ohms in series across a 100-volt, 60 cycle AC supply. The current in this circuit is ______ amperes. 7.____

   A. 2.9  B. 4.0  C. 5.8  D. 8.0

8. A 3-phase, 3-wire, 208-volt, 60-cycle AC service supplies a balanced load consisting of three 30-ohm resistors connected in wye. The line current under these conditions is MOST NEARLY ______ amperes. 8.____

   A. 3.5  B. 4.0  C. 6.9  D. 8.0

9. If the level of the electrolyte in a lead-acid storage battery falls below the top of the plates because of evaporation under normal operating conditions, it is BEST to add 9.____

A. electrolyte
B. sulphuric acid
C. hydrochloric acid
D. water

10. A 600-volt cartridge fuse must have knife blade contacts if its current rating exceeds ______ amperes. 10.____

A. 30 B. 60 C. 80 D. 100

11. When the magnitude of the short circuit currents in a feeder circuit must be limited, this is USUALLY accomplished by means of 11.____

A. resistors
B. reactors
C. capacitors
D. contactors

12. The cross-sectional area in circular mils of a stranded cable having 37 strands, each of which has a diameter of 90 nils, is MOST NEARLY 12.____

A. 81,000 B. 95,000 C. 300,000 D. 942,000

13. A coil having an average diameter of 4 inches is to be made up from a 1,260-ft.-long length of wire. 13.____
The number of turns in this coil will be MOST NEARLY

A. 100 B. 315 C. 1,200 D. 3,780

14. The device commonly known as a *growler* is FREQUENTLY used to 14.____

A. test DC armature windings for shorts
B. clean commutators
C. check insulation of circuit wiring within a raceway
D. sound alarms

15. When a megger is applied alternately to the two leads of a direct-current electrolytic capacitor, the readings will 15.____

A. start and remain at zero for both connections
B. start at zero but increase gradually for one of the connections
C. start at zero but increase gradually for both connections
D. be high at first but decrease gradually for both connections

16. The devices used to convert direct current to alternating current are called 16.____

A. rectifiers
B. transformers
C. rotary converters
D. inverters

17. Of the following conditions, the one which is MOST likely to cause flashing or excessive arcing from brush to brush in a motor is 17.____

A. brushes being set at the improper angle for the direction of rotation
B. brush pressure being too great
C. brushes being too hard
D. excessively high voltage on the line

18. The currents in the armature equalizer connections in a DC generator are 18.____

    A. passed through the brushes
    B. pure DC currents
    C. DC currents containing 120 cycle ripple
    D. alternating currents

19. A generating station has one 1000-Kw and two 2000-Kw generators. 19.____
    To supply 2000 Kw MOST economically, the operating conditions should be

    A. two 2000-Kw generators at half load
    B. one 2000-Kw generator at full load
    C. the 1000-Kw generator at full load and one 2000-Kw generator at half load
    D. the 1000-Kw generator at full load and each of the 2000-Kw generators at 500-Kw load

20. The terminal voltage of a DC shunt generator having an armature current of 100 amperes, an armature resistance of 0.02 ohms, and a generated E.M.F. of 222 volts is MOST NEARLY ______ volts. 20.____

    A. 200  B. 220  C. 224  D. 242

21. The number of poles in the field of an alternator generating voltage at a frequency of 60 cycles per second while rotating at 1200 r.p.m. is 21.____

    A. 4  B. 6  C. 8  D. 12

22. If the field of a shunt motor opens while running, the motor will 22.____

    A. stop running
    B. continue to run at the same speed
    C. slow down
    D. run away

23. To reverse the direction of rotation of a cumulative compound motor, and not have it run as a differential compound motor, reverse the connections to the ______ field. 23.____

    A. shunt
    B. series
    C. shunt field and to the series
    D. armature and to the shunt

24. The MAIN contributing factor to motor stator failure *usually* is 24.____

    A. eddy currents
    B. bearing trouble
    C. dirt
    D. hysteresis

25. The input of a motor is 40,000 watts and its efficiency is 80 percent. 25.____
    The TOTAL energy loss is______ watts.

    A. 32,000  B. 8,000  C. 5,000  D. 2,500

26. The full load current of a three-phase 5 hp motor operating at 200 volts, 60 cycles, and having an efficiency of 80 percent and a power factor of 85 percent is MOST NEARLY ______ amperes. 26.____

    A. 9.7  B. 12.1  C. 14.4  D. 18.0

27. Of the following motors, the one that has the BEST speed regulation is the _______ motor. 27._____

A. series
B. compound
C. shunt
D. split-phase

28. The full load speed of a 60-cycle, 208-volt, 3-phase induction motor having 6 poles and operating with a slip of 10% is MOST NEARLY ______ r.p.m. 28._____

A. 540
B. 600
C. 1080
D. 1200

29. Of the following, a MAJOR advantage of an AC synchronous motor is that it(s) 29._____

A. does not require direct current
B. can be used for power factor correction
C. speed of rotation can be varied by means of a field rheostat
D. can respond to disturbances in the power system by hunting

30. If the field current of a synchronous motor is increased to a point which makes the synchronous motor overexcited, the 30._____

A. power factor will be decreased
B. motor rotational speed will be increased
C. motor rotational speed will be decreased
D. motor will take a leading current

31. When transformers are to be operated in parallel, it is NOT necessary that the transformer have the same 31._____

A. ratio of transformation
B. voltage rating
C. polarity of the terminals that connect together
D. KVA rating

32. A transformer rated at 200 KVA is FULLY loaded with a lagging power factor of 80% when it is supplying 32._____

A. 160 KW
B. 200 KW
C. 250 KVA
D. 80 KVA

33. If the current in the primary of a current transformer is 500 amperes and the transformer has a ratio of 100 to 5, an ammeter connected to the secondary will read MOST NEARLY ______ amperes. 33._____

A. 5
B. 20
C. 25
D. 100

34. Assume that a switchboard ammeter which is connected to a current transformer is damaged and must be removed without interrupting the service.
Of the following, an ESSENTIAL precaution to be taken before disconnecting the ammeter is to 34._____

A. ground the mid-point of the transformer secondary
B. ground one end of the transformer secondary
C. disconnect both ammeter leads simultaneously
D. short the secondary of the transformer

35. A DC relay is rated at 6 volts and 120 ohms. 35.____
This relay can be operated from a 120 volt line by connecting a ______ -ohm resistance in ______ with the relay.

A. 2280; parallel
B. 2280; series
C. 2400; parallel
D. 2400; series

36. Some relays are provided with dash-pots. 36.____
The FUNCTION of these dash-pots is to provide

A. delayed time action
B. instantaneous time action
C. undervoltage protection
D. overcurrent protection

37. An ammeter has a full scale deflection for a current of 0.01 amperes and an internal resistance of 20 ohms. 37.____
In order to have the ammeter read full-scale for a current of 10 amperes and not damage its movement, a shunt should be used having a value of ______ ohms.

A. 10
B. 0.2
C. 0.02
D. 0.01

38. An air circuit breaker has contacts that flash. The MOST probable cause of this trouble is that the 38.____

A. overload relays are set too low
B. contacts are overheating
C. closing-coil circuit is defective
D. barriers are broken

39. The MAIN purpose of a *shunt trip* on a circuit breaker is to 39.____

A. open all phases in a polyphase circuit if there is a failure in any one of the phases
B. prevent phase reversal
C. permit the breaker to be opened electrically from a remote location, regardless of load conditions at the breaker
D. prevent manual tripping

40. The grid-controlled gas-type electronic tube MOST often used in motor control circuits is the 40.____

A. magnetron
B. thyratron
C. ignitron
D. strobatron

---

# KEY (CORRECT ANSWERS)

| | | | | | | | |
|---|---|---|---|---|---|---|---|
| 1. | C | 11. | B | 21. | B | 31. | D |
| 2. | B | 12. | C | 22. | D | 32. | A |
| 3. | B | 13. | C | 23. | C | 33. | C |
| 4. | D | 14. | A | 24. | C | 34. | D |
| 5. | C | 15. | B | 25. | B | 35. | B |
| 6. | A | 16. | D | 26. | C | 36. | A |
| 7. | B | 17. | D | 27. | C | 37. | C |
| 8. | C | 18. | D | 28. | C | 38. | D |
| 9. | D | 19. | B | 29. | B | 39. | C |
| 10. | B | 20. | B | 30. | D | 40. | B |

# TEST 2

DIRECTIONS: Each question or incomplete statement is followed by several suggested answers or completions. Select the one that BEST answers the question or completes the statement. *PRINT THE LETTER OF THE CORRECT ANSWER IN THE SPACE AT THE RIGHT.*

1. Under normal atmospheric conditions, a pressure gauge that reads 24 inches of mercury is indicating an *absolute pressure* of MOST NEARLY _____ P.S.I. 1.____

   A. 26.5 B. 14.7 C. 11.8 D. 8.7

2. The PRIMARY function of a hygrometer is to measure 2.____

   A. relative humidity
   B. specific gravity
   C. liquid levels
   D. pressure differentials

3. A venturi meter is used to measure the rate of 3.____

   A. vibration of engine footings
   B. electric power consumption
   C. heat transfer
   D. fluid flow

4. The PRINCIPAL thickening agent used in lubricating greases is 4.____

   A. metallic soap
   B. olein
   C. palmitin
   D. lecithin

5. The specific gravity of liquids is USUALLY determined by means of a 5.____

   A. bolometer
   B. calorimeter
   C. fathometer
   D. hydrometer

6. The pull required on the fall line (neglecting friction) to hoist a 120-pound weight, using a four-part block and tackle, is _____ lbs. 6.____

   A. 30 B. 60 C. 80 D. 100

7. Of the following terms, the one which does NOT describe a way of finishing the ends of a rope is the 7.____

   A. eye splice
   B. backlash
   C. whip
   D. bight

8. When hoisting a load by means of a sling, the stress in each leg of the sling will 8.____

   A. increase as the angle between the horizontal and the sling leg decreases
   B. decrease as the angle between the horizontal and the sling leg decreases
   C. increase as the angle between the horizontal and the sling leg increases
   D. be independent of the angle between the horizontal and the sling leg

9. The MAXIMUM pressure in an upright cylinder 6 feet in diameter, 8 feet high, and open at the top, when filled to the brim with water, is MOST NEARLY _____ lbs/sq.ft. 9.____

   A. 250 B. 375 C. 500 D. 750

10. The MAXIMUM height to which water can be lifted by means of suction alone, at sea level, is APPROXIMATELY ______ feet. 10.____

A. 10 B. 22 C. 34 D. 47

11. The TOTAL number of 4-inch diameter pipes that is required to equal the water flow capacity of an 8-inch diarieter pipe (neglecting friction) is 11.____

A. 2 B. 3 C. 4 D. 5

12. The number of threads, per inch, on the standard machine screw MOST suitable for general use is 12.____

A. 50 B. 32 C. 17 D. 10

13. The friction losses which occur when water flows through a pipe vary MOST NEARLY ______ with the ______ . 13.____

A. *directly*; velocity squared
B. *inversely*; velocity squared
C. *directly*; velocity
D. *inversely*; velocity

14. Small by-pass lines are sometimes furnished around large gate valves MAINLY to 14.____

A. balance the pressure on the gate when the valve is being opened
B. permit dumping of the excess fluid
C. meter the flow
D. divert fluid in case the valve becomes stuck

15. The sudden surge caused by an abrupt change in the speed of the pumps in a closed liquid piping system is USUALLY called 15.____

A. tailing B. water hammer
C. precipitation D. jetting

16. The valve that permits water to flow in one direction only is the ______ valve. 16.____

A. gate B. globe C. angle D. check

17. Most flanged butterfly valves can be brought from a fully closed position to a fully opened position in ______ turn(s). 17.____

A. two full B. one full
C. a half D. a quarter

18. The efficiency of two centrifugal pumps operating in parallel is ______ of one of the pumps operating alone. 18.____

A. one-half that
B. practically the same as that
C. twice that
D. four times that

19. Assume that a spur gear having 20 teeth revolves at 80 r.p.m. and drives another spur gear having 40 teeth. The speed at which the gear having 40 teeth revolves is _______ r.p.m. 19.____

A. 160 B. 40 C. 20 D. 10

20. A centrifugal pump has a plain flat-joint seal between the impeller and the casing. If the clearance of the seal becomes enlarged due to wear, thereby reducing the pump's efficiency, it would be GOOD practice to 20.____

A. tighten down on the casing
B. use the pumps only in an emergency
C. replace the wearing ring
D. renew the impeller

21. The one of the following statements which CORRECTLY describes a speed characteristic for a centrifugal pump under normal operating conditions is: 21.____

A. Capacity varies directly with the square of the speed
B. Total head varies directly with the square of the speed
C. Fluid power varies directly with the square of the speed
D. Fluid power varies directly with the speed

22. The MAIN function of a pump stuffing box is to 22.____

A. protect the pump against leakage at the point where the shaft passes through the pump casing
B. provide a ball bearing race
C. couple the pump to its motor
D. prime the pump

23. The PROPER order of the events that take place in a 4-stroke internal combustion engine is: 23.____

A. Air intake, power expansion, compression, and exhaust
B. Power expansion, air intake, compression, and exhaust
C. Air intake, compression, power expansion, and exhaust
D.

24. The number of cycles in an internal combustion engine is AT LEAST _______ cycles. 24.____

A. two B. three C. four D. five

25. The lumens per watt taken by a lamp varies with the type and size of lamp. Given that a one candlepower light source emits 12.57 lumens, the lumens per watt taken by a 75 candlepower lamp drawing 40 watts is APPROXIMATELY 25.____

A. 1.9 B. 6.7 C. 23.6 D. 240

26. A 230-volt, 25-cycle magnetic brake coil is to be rewound to operate properly on 60 cycles at the same voltage. Assuming that the coil at 25-cycles has 1800 turns, at 60 cycles the number of turns should be 26.____

A. reduced to 750 B. increased to 2400
C. reduced to 420 D. increased to 3000

27. Nichrome wire having a resistance of 200 ohms per 100 feet is to be used for a heater requiring a total resistance of 10 ohms. 27.____
The length, in feet, of wire required is

A. 5 B. 15 C. 25 D. 50

28. The MAIN reason for grounding conduit is to prevent the conduit from becoming 28.____

A. corroded by electrolysis
B. magnetized
C. a source of radio interference
D. accidentally energized at a higher potential than ground

29. A feeder consisting of a positive and a negative wire supplies a motor load. The feeder is connected to bus-bars having a constant potential of 230 volts. The feeder is 500 ft. long and consists of two 250,000 circular-mil conductors. The maximum load on the feeder is 170 amps. Assume that the resistance of 1000 ft. of this cable is 0.0431 ohm. 29.____
The voltage, at the motor terminals, is MOST NEARLY

A. 201V B. 209V C. 213V D. 217V

30. With reference to Question 29, the efficiency of transmission, in percent, is MOST NEARLY 30.____

A. 83% B. 87% C. 91% D. 97%

31. With reference to AC motors, in addition to overload, many other things cause fuses to blow. 31.____
The fuse will blow if, in starting an AC motor, the operator throws the starting switch of the compensator to the running position

A. too slowly
B. too quickly
C. with main switch in open position
D. with main switch in closed position

32. A change in speed of a DC motor of 10 to 15 percent can USUALLY be made by 32.____

A. rewinding the armature
B. rewinding the field
C. decreasing the number of turns in the field coils
D. increasing or decreasing the gap between the armature and field

33. Of the following types of fire extinguishers, the one MOST suitable for use on fires in electrical equipment is the ______ extinguisher. 33.____

A. soda-acid
B. loaded stream
C. foam
D. dry chemical

34. Portable fire extinguishers suitable for use on electrical fires are USUALLY identified by a label with the following symbol______ in a ______. 34.____

A. *A*; triangle
B. *B*; square
C. *C*; circle
D. *D*; five-pointed star

35. When flammable liquids are poured from one container to another, a bond wire is sometimes connected between the containers to 35.____

A. prevent the liquid from spilling
B. prevent the containers from dropping
C. ensure that the containers will be sealed after pouring is completed
D. eliminate sparks due to static electricity

36. The proper way to lift a heavy object includes all of the following techniques EXCEPT 36.____

A. placing the feet as far away from the object as possible
B. bending the knees
C. keeping the back straight
D. lifting with the arm and leg muscles

37. The contents of different piping systems are sometimes identified by means of standard color codes, such as the one recommended by the American National Standards Institute (formerly the American Standards Institute). According to this Institute's standards, a piping system used for fire protection should be designated by the color 37.____

A. green B. blue C. red D. yellow

38. Assume that the contents of a container are described as *TOXIC.* This means they are 38.____

A. explosive
B. fragile
C. poisonous
D. volatile

39. An authoritative source of emergency information on antidotes is the 39.____

A. Fire Department
B. Poison Control Center, Department of Health
C. public library
D. National Labor Relations Board

40. Unexpected operation of electrical equipment that can be started by remote control may cause injury to workers making repairs.
Before making repairs on such equipment, it is GOOD practice to 40.____

A. follow a lockout procedure
B. bypass the interlocks
C. ground all live conductors
D. uncouple all motors

# KEY (CORRECT ANSWERS)

| | | | | | | | |
|---|---|---|---|---|---|---|---|
| 1. | A | 11. | C | 21. | B | 31. | B |
| 2. | A | 12. | B | 22. | A | 32. | D |
| 3. | D | 13. | A | 23. | C | 33. | D |
| 4. | A | 14. | A | 24. | A | 34. | C |
| 5. | D | 15. | B | 25. | C | 35. | D |
| 6. | A | 16. | D | 26. | A | 36. | A |
| 7. | D | 17. | D | 27. | D | 37. | C |
| 8. | A | 18. | B | 28. | D | 38. | C |
| 9. | C | 19. | B | 29. | D | 39. | B |
| 10. | C | 20. | D | 30. | D | 40. | A |

---

# EXAMINATION SECTION
# TEST 1

DIRECTIONS: Each question or incomplete statement is followed by several suggested answers or completions. Select the one that BEST answers the question or completes the statement. *PRINT THE LETTER OF THE CORRECT ANSWER IN THE SPACE AT THE RIGHT.*

1. Assume that an engine has a no-load speed of 1800 RPM and a full-load speed of 1650 RPM, 1____
   The speed regulation of this engine is MOST NEARLY

   A. 12%. B. 11% C. 9.1% D. 8.4%

2. The color of the third wire used for grounding portable electric power tools is generally 2____

   A. black B. white C. red D. green

3. A series circuit consists of a pure inductance and a pure resistance. When an AC voltage is impressed across such a circuit, the ______ the resistence by 90 degrees. 3____

   A. current in the inductance lags the current in
   B. current in the inductance leads the current in
   C. voltage across the inductance lags the voltage across
   D. voltage across the inductance leads the voltage across

4. Of the following devices, the one which should be used for throttling of water going through it is the ______ valve. 4____

   A. gate B. globe C. check D. relief

5. If the line-to-line voltage of a wye-connected 3-phase system is 220 volts AC and the phase current is 10 amperes, then the total power delivered is MOST NEARLY ______ watts. 5____

   A. 1270 B. 2200 C. 3800 D. 6600

6. The sensitivity of a meter movement is given as 50 microamperes. This is equivalent to a voltmeter rating of ______ ohms/volt. 6____

   A. 50,000 B. 20,000 C. 50 D. 20

7. Doubling the number of turns of an inductor should ______ its original value. 7____

   A. *reduce* the inductance to one-quarter of
   B. *reduce* the inductance to one-half of
   C. *increase* the inductance to twice
   D. *increase* the inductance to four times

8. Electrical fuses are rated in 8____

   A. current and voltage B. current and wattage
   C. ampere-hours D. watt-hours

9. A 30-ohm resistor is placed in parallel with an inductor that has an inductive reactance of 40 ohms. If 120 volts AC is impressed across the parallel combination, the *total current* drawn from the 120-volt AC line is ______ amps. 9____

A. 1.7 B. 2.4 C. 3.0 D. 5.0

10. The symbol shown at the right, found in the schematic of a motor control circuit represents a 10____

A. silicon-controlled rectifier
B. thyratron
C. heat-sunk diode
D. thermal overload

11. A device that can be used to check the condition of the electrolyte in a storage battery is the 11____

A. hygrometer B. hydrometer
C. hydrostat D. aquastat

12. Of the following, the BEST device to use to check the condition of the insulation of a cable is the 12____

A. ohmmeter B. wheatstone bridge
C. voltmeter D. megger

13. The decibel is a unit used in measuring the level of 13____

A. magnetization B. acidity
C. sound D. contamination

14. A rectangular bus bar with a cross-section of.1.0 inch x .50 inch has a cross-sectional area MOST NEARLY equivalent to ______ circular mils. 14____

A. 250,000 B. 640,000
C. 1,000,000 D. 1,280,000

15. The electrical conductivity of copper is lower than that of 15____

A. silver B. gold C. carbon D. aluminum

16. A voltmeter has a ground connection and two terminals, one of which is used for 0-300 volts and the other for 0-750 volts. The scale is marked only for the 0-750 range. A scale reading of 200, when the 0-300 volt range is being used, corresponds to an actual voltage of ______ volts. 16____

A. 200 B. 160 C. 120 D. 80

17. When putting out a fire with a hand extinguisher, it is BEST to direct the discharge at the ______ the fire. 17____

A. base of B. area behind
C. area in front of D. highest flames of

18. Someone suggests that the silver-plated main contacts of a circuit breaker be cleaned with fine sandpaper. This suggestion is 18____

A. *poor,* since the useful silver plating would be removed
B. *good,* since you would be removing silver oxide which is a poor conductor
C. *good,* since this will prevent overheating of the circuit breaker
D. *poor,* since this will change the adjustment of the main contacts

19. If a multi-scale DC voltmeter reads downscale (goes below zero) when connected across two pins of an electrical connector, it is MOST likely that the 19____

A. meter is defective
B. voltage across the pins is AC
C. meter leads are reversed
D. wrong scale is being used

20. Measurements of illumination in a work area are made with light meters which measure in units of 20____

A. foot-lamberts
B. foot-candles
C. lumens
D. watts

21. Assume that new types of circuit breakers and controls are to be installed in the plant where you work. This equipment is to be operated and maintained by you. Of the following, the FIRST step you should take to become familiar with the new equipment is to 21____

A. read the instruction books for the equipment
B. call in the manufacturer's field personnel for instructions
C. read textbooks on the general theory of such equipment
D. make trial disassemblies and reassemblies of the equipment

22. Of the following, the BEST way to lift a heavy object is to 22____

A. keep legs spread apart and straight, slowly bending at the waist to grasp the object
B. place the feet about shoulder-width apart and slowly bend at the knees to reach down to the object
C. keep legs straight and close together, slowly bending at the waist to grasp the object
D. place feet close together, and with legs and back straight, bend at the waist to reach down and quickly lift the object

23. Sparks and open flames should be kept away from storage batteries that are being charged because of the high combustibility of the 23____

A. electrolytes in the batteries
B. battery cases when hot
C. gases being produced
D. sulfuric acid fumes being generated

24. A 16-foot wood ladder is to be leaned against a wall. Of the following, the SAFEST distance at which the base of the ladder should be placed from the base of the wall is ______ feet. 24____

A. 4
B. 6
C. 8
D. 9

25. Of the following fittings, the one used to connect two lengths of conduit in a straight line is a(n) 25____

A. elbow B. nipple C. tee D. coupling

26. If a nut is to be tightened to an exact specified value, the wrench that should be used is a(n) ______ wrench. 26____

A. torque B. lock-j aw C. alligator D. spanner

27. Unloaders are generally found on 27____

A. centrifugal pumps
B. air compressors
C. flexible couplings
D. surge suppressors

28. A compound gauge indicates 28____

A. pressures in lbs. and vacuums in inches of water
B. both pressures and vacuums in lbs. per sq. inch
C. pressures in lbs. per sq. inch and vacuums in inches of mercury
D. pressures in lbs. and vacuums in inches of mercury per sq. inch

29. Of the following, the metal that is used for bearing linings is 29____

A. Muntz metal
B. duraluminum
C. naval brass
D. babbitt

30. It has been discovered that the commutator of an electrical machine has developed a flat spot. 30____
To remove the flat spot, the

A. entire commutator should be ground or turned down until the flat spot is removed
B. brushes should be changed to a harder grade and the flat spot will eventually wear away
C. entire commutator should be resurfaced with emery cloth attached to a wooden block which is then pressed against the turning commutator
D. commutator bars that have the flat spot should be removed for repair or replacement, then reassembled back into the commutator

31. The FIRST operation performed on raw sewage as it comes into a sewage treatment plant is to 31____

A. add sufficient amounts of chlorine to kill any living organisms
B. place it into settling tanks to allow sludge to settle to the bottom
C. pass it through screens to remove or break up coarse material
D. introduce selected bacteria to initiate biodegrada-tion

32. The MAIN function of diffusers in sewage treatment plants is to 32____

A. maintain a uniform distribution of non-solubles in the sewage
B. release compressed air into the sewage
C. pass the sewage through a fine filter
D. disperse objectionable and toxic gases that are formed in the sewage

33. A comminutor at a sewage plant is used to 33____

A. shred sewage matter that is not removed by screens
B. enable people in one building to talk to people in other buildings
C. convert AC electric power to DC in the sewage plant
D. reduce the level of noise in the sewage settling basin building

34. The pH of a substance is an indication of its 34____

A. resistance to corrosion
B. magnetic properties
C. transparency or translucency
D. acidity or alkalinity

35. Assume that a vacuum gauge reads 15 inches of Hg. The equivalent in *absolute pressure* is MOST NEARLY ______ p.s.i. 35____

A. 2.0 B. 4.0 C. 7.5 D. 14.7

---

# KEY (CORRECT ANSWERS)

1. C
2. D
3. D
4. B
5. C

6. B
7. D
8. A
9. D
10. A

11. B
12. D
13. C
14. B
15. A

16. D
17. A
18. A
19. C
20. B

21. A
22. B
23. C
24. A
25. D

26. A
27. B
28. C
29. D
30. A

31. C
32. B
33. A
34. D
35. C

---

# TEST 2

DIRECTIONS: Each question or incomplete statement is followed by several suggested answers or completions. Select the one that BEST answers the question or completes the statement. *PRINT THE LETTER OF THE CORRECT ANSWER IN THE SPACE AT THE RIGHT.*

1. An ADVANTAGE of a rotary pump over a centrifugal pump is that the rotary pump is 1____

   A. self-priming and requires no valves
   B. better able to handle gritty water
   C. better suited for high pressures and high discharges
   D. quieter and has a pulseless discharge

2. A method used to eliminate water hammer in a water line is to 2____

   A. increase the pressure in the line
   B. use slow-closing valves and faucets
   C. treat the water with a water softener
   D. increase the temperature of the water

3. A pipe nipple that is threaded over its entire length is called a _______ nipple. 3____

   A. shoulder B. long C. close D. short

4. A Stillson wrench is also called a _______ wrench. 4____

   A. strap B. pipe C. monkey D. crescent

5. In a piping diagram, the symbol shown at the right represents a 5____

   A. pressure regulator B. strainer
   C. check valve D. drier

6. A shut-off valve is found to have the designation *WOG 300*. The letters WOG mean 6____

   A. Water or Gas Valve
   B. Water, Oil or Gas Pressure
   C. Worthington Gate Valve
   D. Working Gauge Pressure

7. A plunger-type compressed-air-driven reciprocating water pump has a marking *3x4x7*. The number *7* refers to the 7____

   A. diameter of the compressed air piston in inches
   B. diameter of the water piston in inches
   C. length of the stroke in inches
   D. compression ratio

8. Methane is a gas that 8____

   A. has a smell like rotten eggs
   B. is heavier than air
   C. forms the major part of natural gas
   D. is non-combustible

9. As a cylinder in a diesel engine is going through its compression cycle, the air in the cylinder will _______ in pressure and _______ in temperature. 9_____

A. *decrease; decrease* B. *increase; increase*
C. decrease; increase D. *increase; decrease*

10. A specification for the installation of a storage tank indicates that a hydrostatic test should be made before placing the tank in service. 10_____
A hydrostatic test consists of

A. immersing the tank, with ports closed, in water and checking for water seeping in
B. filling the tank with water under pressure and noting how well the pressure is held or whether water leaks out
C. creating a vacuum in the interior of the tank and noting how well the vacuum is held or whether air leaks in
D. filling the tank with compressed air and checking for leaks with soapy water

11. When the ignition characteristics of a fuel are represented by a cetane number, the fuel is one that is normally used in a 11_____

A. gasoline engine B. gas turbine
C. diesel engine D. steam boiler

12. Of the following, a characteristic of a wound-rotor AC induction motor is that it 12_____

A. provides a wide range of speed control
B. does not require slip-rings
C. has a *squirrel cage* armature
D. operates on single-phase power

13. Detergents are used in lubricating oils to 13_____

A. reduce the S.A.E. number
B. prevent oxidation of the oil
C. keep insoluble matter in suspension
D. combat corrosion

14. In a four-stroke diesel engine, each piston fires every _______ of the crankshaft. 14_____

A. one-half revolution B. revolution
C. two revolutions D. four revolutions

15. An electric motor with pressure grease fittings and relief plugs requires lubrication, A grease gun should be connected to each fitting and the grease gun should be pumped *until* 15_____

A. grease oozes out along the shaft
B. grease oozes out from the relief plug hole
C. the handle becomes hard to move
D. the handle starts to move freely

16. Of the following, the one which is NOT used for applying grease to a bearing is a(n) 16_____

A. Alemite fitting B. grease cup
C. Zerk fitting D. pressure plug

17. Of the following, the substance that should be used to melt ice on pavements and walkways is called 17____

A. calcium chloride
B. trichloroethylene
C. sodium hydroxide
D. slaked lime

18. On a working drawing, the symbol (shading) given as shown at the right represents 18____

A. cast iron
B. concrete
C. glass
D. steel

19. A machine screw is indicated on a drawing as The head is the American Standard type called _______ head. 19____

A. flat
B. oval
C. fillister
D. round

20. The tool that is shown at the right is properly referred to as a(n) ______ tap. 20____

A. bottoming
B. acme
C. taper
D. plug

21. The tool indicated at the right is referred to as an arch punch.
This tool should be used to 21____

A. cut holes in 1/16 inch steel
B. cut large diameter holes in masonry
C. run through a conduit prior to pulling a cable or wires
D. make holes in rubber or leather gasket material

22. Before putting an aerosol container for garbage pickup, it is *good* practice to 22____

A. puncture it with a screwdriver
B. use out the contents in normal manner
C. put it out as is regardless of container contents
D. remove the spray nozzle

23. A lantern ring is a type of 23____

A. optical illusion on a light source seen through a fine screen mesh
B. sealing arrangement used to minimize air leakage between a rotating shaft and a sleeve
C. piston ring which provides lubrication of the cylinder wall
D. oil ring bearing lubrication

24. Monel metal is an alloy used for water heater tanks. It is a combination MAINLY of 24____

A. iron and lead
B. chromium and zinc
C. nickel and copper
D. vanadium and tin

25. The plumbing fitting shown at the right is called a 25____

A. Street Elbow
B. Return Bend
C. Running Trap
D. Reversing *El*

26. A galvanized steel plate is a plate with a coating of 26____

A. lead and tin alloy
B. tin
C. zinc
D. brass

27. *If* the barrel of a standard micrometer is rotated through one complete revolution, the *gap* dimension is changed by ______ inch, 27____

A. .010
B. .025
C. .100
D. .250

28. Of the following, the indication that a fluorescent lamp is in need of replacement is that 28____

A. a very low level hum is produced by the ballast
B. there is a slight delay before the lamp comes up to full brightness after the switch is turned on
C. the lamp flashes on and off, and there are black coatings at the ends
D. the lamp does not go off each time the switch is turned off

29. The one of the following that is recommended for prime-coating bare metals is 29____

A. varnish
B. zinc chromate
C. shellac
D. linseed oil

30. *Dressing* a grinding wheel refers to 30____

A. replacing the wheel with a new one
B. reducing the thickness of the wheel
C. cleaning the grinding surface and making the wheel round
D. repositioning the wheel on its shaft to eliminate *wobble*

31. A fusible metal plug is a protective device that 31____

A. melts when the electric current through it exceeds the rating
B. melts when its temperature reaches a specific figure
C. ruptures when the pressure behind it goes beyond a certain level
D. ruptures when the *pull* on it exceeds a specified number of pounds

32. Of the following, the material that is beginning to be used for electrical conduits, plastic water pipes, and electrical insulation is 32____

A. trichloroethyline
B. polyvinylchloride
C. carbontrichlorofluoride
D. teflon

33. At certain conditions of speed, pressure, and temperature, centrifugal pumps can be made to cavitate. 33____
The conditions causing cavitation

A. should be avoided since the impeller may become seriously pitted
B. result in the highest pump efficiency
C. produce *water hammer* and should be avoided
D. also produce the quietest operation of the pump

34. A nut is turned on a 1/2" - 10 bolt. 34____
When the nut is turned through five complete turns on the bolt, the distance it moves longitudinally on the bolt is ______ inch.

A. .100 B. .200 C. .375 D. .500

35. A growler is a device used for 35____

A. vibrating pipes carrying solid matter
B. sounding an alarm when hazardous conditions develop
C. detecting shorts in armatures
D. chewing up solids in sewage

---

## KEY (CORRECT ANSWERS)

1. A
2. B
3. C
4. B
5. C

6. B
7. C
8. C
9. B
10. B

11. C
12. A
13. C
14. C
15. B

16. D
17. A
18. D
19. B
20. A

21. D
22. B
23. B
24. C
25. B

26. C
27. B
28. C
29. B
30. C

31. B
32. B
33. A
34. D
35. C

---

# EXAMINATION SECTION
# TEST 1

DIRECTIONS: Each question or incomplete statement is followed by several suggested answers or completions. Select the one that BEST answers the question or completes the statement. *PRINT THE LETTER OF THE CORRECT ANSWER IN THE SPACE AT THE RIGHT.*

1. The direction of rotation of a d.c. shunt motor can be reversed by reversing 1.____

   A. the line leads
   B. both the armature and field current
   C. the field or armature current
   D. the current in one pole winding

2. The insulation resistance of the stator winding of an induction motor is MOST commonly measured or tested with a(n) 2.____

   A. strobe B. ammeter C. megger D. S-meter

3. Assume that three 12-ohm resistances are connected in delta across a 208-volt, 3-phase circuit. The line current, in amperes, will be MOST NEARLY 3.____

   A. 30 B. 20.4 C. 17.32 D. 8.66

4. Assume that three 12 ohm resistances are connected in wye across a 208-volt, 3-phase circuit. The power, in watts, dissipated in this resistance load will be MOST NEARLY 4.____

   A. 4200 B. 3600 C. 1200 D. 900

5. The one of the following knots which is MOST commonly used to shorten a rope without cutting it is the 5.____

   A. clove hitch B. diamond knot
   C. sheepshank D. square knot

6. Assume that it is required to pump 40 M.G.D. of water against a 65 ft. head. If the pump efficiency is 65%, the B.H.P. of this pump is MOST NEARLY 6.____

   A. 920 B. 700 C. 460 D. 176

7. Assume that a pump had to be shut down temporarily due to trouble which was first reported by an oiler. The one of the following entries in the log concerning this occurrence which is LEAST important is the 7.____

   A. time of the shutdown
   B. period of time the pump was out of service
   C. cause of the trouble
   D. time the oiler came on shift

8. At sea level, the theoretical maximum distance, in feet, that water can be lifted by suction only is MOST NEARLY 8.____

   A. 12.00 B. 14.70 C. 33.57 D. 72.0

9. While a lubricating oil is in use, for good performance, its neutralization number should 9.____

A. keep rising
B. remain about the same
C. be greater than 0.1
D. be greater than 2.0

10. Cast iron castings that need repairing are USUALLY repaired by the process known as 10.____

A. electric arc welding
B. electro-forming
C. brazing
D. resistance welding

11. The term SAE stands for 11.____

A. Standard Auto Engines
B. Standard Air Engines
C. Society of Automotive Engineers
D. Society of Aviation Engineers

12. The parts of a large sewage pump that would MOST likely need repairs after the least number of hours of operation are the 12.____

A. pump casings
B. impellers
C. wearing rings
D. outboard bearings

13. Assume that the power in a balanced three-phase load is measured by the two wattmeter method and is read by means of two wattmeters, namely $W_1$ and $W_2$. If the power factor of the load is .5 leading, 13.____

A. $W_1$ will read positive and $W_2$ will read negative
B. $W_1$ will read negative and $W_2$ will read positive
C. both $W_1$ and $W_2$ will read negative
D. $W_1$ will read positive and $W_2$ will read zero

14. The current in amperes of a 220-volt 5-H.P., d.c. motor having an efficiency of 90% is MOST NEARLY 14.____

A. 18.8
B. 17
C. 14.3
D. 20.5

15. A shunt generator having an armature current of 50 amperes, an armature resistance of .05 ohms, and a generated e.m.f. of 222.5 volts will MOST likely have a terminal voltage of ______ volts. 15.____

A. 172.5
B. 220.0
C. 222.5
D. 225

16. Assume that a 4-pole, 220-volt d.c. motor has a back e.m.f. of 215 volts and 4 armature paths between terminals. If the field flux per pole is suddenly decreased to one-half of its former value, the motor speed, in r.p.m., compared to its original speed will be MOST likely 16.____

A. decreased to about one-quarter
B. decreased to about one-half
C. doubled
D. increased by one-quarter

17. The frequency of the voltage generated in a synchronous machine having 8 poles and running at 720 r.p.m. is MOST NEARLY 17.____

A. 120 B. 72 C. 60 D. 48

18. Assume that a synchronous converter has two slip rings and a direct current voltage of 313 volts between the brushes. The effective alternating voltage between slip rings is MOST NEARLY _______ volts. 18.____

A. 220 B. 278 C. 330 D. 440

19. A newly appointed plant engineer attempted to make an emergency repair on a d.c. motor which had an open armature coil (lap wound) by completely cutting this coil in two and disconnecting it from both commutator bars and then running an insulated jumper large enough to safely carry the current between the two bars. This attempted emergency repair will 19.____

A. result in an inoperative motor
B. not significantly affect the normal running of the motor
C. cause the motor to emit vicious purplish sparks at the commutator while running
D. cause the motor to overheat excessively while running

20. The purpose of full wave rectifiers is to 20.____

A. produce a.c. current which contains some d.c.
B. change d.c. current to a.c.
C. produce d.c. current having an a.c. ripple of twice the input frequency
D. produce only a.c. current having twice the input frequency

21. The temporary production of a substitute for a two-phase current so as to obtain a makeshift rotating field in starting a single phase motor is called 21.____

A. phase splitting B. pole pitch
C. phase transformation D. pole splitting

22. In a fully charged lead acid storage battery, the active material in the positive plates is 22.____

A. sponge lead B. lead carbonate
C. lead acetate D. lead peroxide

23. A heat exchanger commonly located between the low pressure and high pressure cylinders of an air compressor is used to _______ of the compressor air. 23.____

A. lower the temperature
B. increase the relative humidity
C. decrease the relative humidity
D. raise the temperature

24. The one of the following instruments which is used for the determination of the velocity of air in ducts is the 24.____

A. psychrometer B. pitot tube
C. *U* gage D. spherometer

25. A high tension breaker (4160 volts) should be equipped with a mechanical interlock which will prevent the breaker from being raised or advanced into, and lowered or withdrawn from, the operating position unless 25.____

A. it is open
B. it is closed
C. the full load is connected
D. a light load is connected

26. For the operation of a high tension breaker (4160 volts), the suitable control voltage for BEST performance is usually 26.____

A. 600 volts a.c.
B. 600 volts d.c.
C. 208 to 440 volts a.c.
D. 70 to 140 volts d.c.

27. The equipment on which you would be MOST likely to find an unloader is a(n) 27.____

A. centrifugal water pump
B. air compressor
C. vacuum pump
D. steam engine

28. The term Saybolt refers to a measure of 28.____

A. specific gravity
B. boiling point
C. hardness
D. viscosity

29. Assume that a centrifugal fan running at 750 r.p.m. delivers 20,000 c.f.m. at a static pressure of one inch. If this fan is required to deliver 28,000 c.f.m., at the same static pressure, it should be run at a speed, in r.p.m., of MOST NEARLY 29.____

A. 1500 B. 1250 C. 1150 D. 1050

30. The horsepower of a fan varies as the ______ of the fan speed. 30.____

A. cube
B. square
C. square root
D. cube root

31. The gearing for transmitting power between two shafts at right angles to each other consists of two essential parts: 31.____

A. two worm wheels
B. a worm and bevel gear
C. a rack and pinion
D. two bevel gears

32. If a transmission main drive gear, having 30 teeth, rotates at 400 r.p.m. and drives a counter shaft gear at 300 r.p.m., the total number of teeth on the countershaft drive will be 32.____

A. 30 B. 40 C. 60 D. 80

33. The one of the following faults of a C.B. main contact which is NOT a cause of overheating of air circuit breakers is 33.____

A. excessive pressure
B. insufficient area in contact
C. oxidized contacts
D. dirty contacts

34. The MAIN reason that larger size electrical cables (such as #0000) are always stranded rather than solid is that they 34.____

A. are more flexible
B. are stronger
C. have a higher conductivity
D. have a higher specific resistance

Questions 35-37.

DIRECTIONS: Questions 35 through 37, inclusive, are to be answered in accordance with the diagram of the auto transformer and data below.

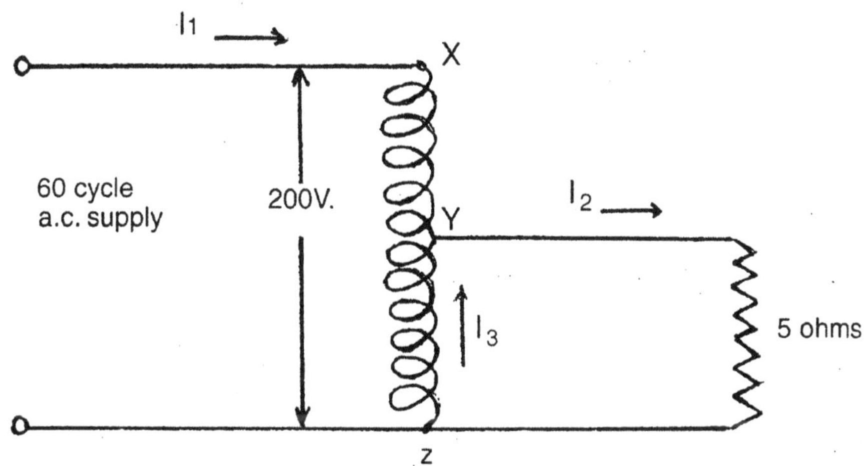


Data: An auto transformer whose primary is XZ is connected across a 200-volt a.c. supply as shown in the above diagram. The load of 5 ohms is connected across Y and Z. (Assume that point Y is the mid-point of the winding.)

35. The current $I_1$, in amperes, is APPROXIMATELY equal to 35.____

A. 5 B. 10 C. 15 D. 20

36. The current $I_2$, in amperes, is APPROXIMATELY equal to 36.____

A. 5 B. 10 C. 15 D. 20

37. The current $I_3$, in amperes, is APPROXIMATELY equal to 37.____

A. 5 B. 10 C. 15 D. 20

38. Assume that you see one of your oilers tumble down a long flight of concrete steps and fall heavily on the lower landing. You rush to him and find that he is unconscious but breathing. Of the following, the BEST course of action for you to take is 38.____

A. have two of your men carry him to the office and summon a doctor
B. do not move him but cover him with a blanket and call a doctor
C. prop him upright and let him inhale spirits of ammonia and call a doctor
D. prepare a bed of blankets and have two of your men lift him on it, then summon a doctor

39. It is sometimes desirable to have a control that will cause a d.c. motor to come to a standstill quickly instead of coasting to a standstill after the stop button is pressed. This result is MOST commonly obtained by means of an action called 39._____

A. counter e.m.f. method
B. armature reaction
C. diverting
D. dynamic braking

40. In an electric circuit, a high-spot-temperature is MOST commonly due to 40._____

A. an open circuit
B. a defective connection
C. intermittent use of circuit
D. excessive distribution voltage

---

## KEY (CORRECT ANSWERS)

| | | | |
|---|---|---|---|
| 1. C | 11. C | 21. A | 31. D |
| 2. C | 12. C | 22. D | 32. B |
| 3. A | 13. D | 23. A | 33. A |
| 4. B | 14. A | 24. B | 34. A |
| 5. C | 15. B | 25. A | 35. B |
| 6. B | 16. C | 26. D | 36. D |
| 7. D | 17. D | 27. B | 37. B |
| 8. C | 18. A | 28. D | 38. B |
| 9. B | 19. B | 29. D | 39. D |
| 10. C | 20. C | 30. A | 40. B |

---

# TEST 2

DIRECTIONS: Each question or incomplete statement is followed by several suggested answers or completions. Select the one that BEST answers the question or completes the statement. *PRINT THE LETTER OF THE CORRECT ANSWER IN THE SPACE AT THE RIGHT.*

1. The MAIN reason for periodic inspections and testing of equipment in an electrically powered plant is to 1.____

   A. keep the men busy at all times
   B. familiarize the men with the equipment
   C. train the men to be ready in an emergency
   D. discover minor faults before they have a chance to become significantly serious

2. Assume that an employee calls up to give advance notice of his intentions to be absent the following day. The MOST important information that he should give is 2.____

   A. the exact time of calling
   B. the balance of his sick leave time
   C. the reason for his absence
   D. name of attending doctor

3. The MAIN reason why a plant mechanic who is assigned to service equipment must be able to make proper adjustments and repairs quickly is that 3.____

   A. equipment always deteriorates rapidly unless readjusted immediately
   B. idle equipment will result in poor plant efficiency and work delays
   C. the ability to work rapidly is the result of extensive training and experience
   D. he will have more time for his other duties

4. A 1300-volt, three-phase system with a grounded neutral has a phase to ground voltage of APPROXIMATELY 4.____

   A. 440 B. 600 C. 690 D. 750

5. A 220-volt, 40-H.P. induction motor is given an insulation resistance test. The normal value of the insulating resistance, in megohms, for this motor is MOST NEARLY 5.____

   A. 0.2 B. 0.4 C. 0.05 D. 0.95

6. To increase the range of an a.c. ammeter, the one of the following which is MOST commonly used is a(n) 6.____

   A. current transformer B. inductance
   C. condenser D. straight copper bar

7. When batteries are being charged, they should not be exposed to open flames and sparks because of the flammability of 7.____

   A. hydrogen B. oxygen
   C. sulphurous gas D. fuming sulphuric acid

8. Assume that you and your supervisor are on an inspectional tour of the outdoor equipment of the plant and that a co-worker suddenly falls unconscious on the pavement. If on close observation you find that the victim is not breathing, the FIRST of the following things to do is 8.____

   A. move the victim indoors
   B. notify his family
   C. administer first aid to restore breathing
   D. nothing, but summon a doctor

9. Assume that one of your men, who has always been efficient, industrious, and conscientious, suddenly becomes lax in his work, makes numerous mistakes, and shuns responsibilities. The cause of such a change 9.____

   A. is usually that the man is responding to a minor change in the job situation
   B. is usually apparent to the stationary engineer in charge and fellow workers
   C. may be quickly found by a close study of reports and personnel records
   D. may have no direct relationship to any change in the job situation

Questions 10-12.

DIRECTIONS: Questions 10 through 12, inclusive, are to be answered in accordance with the diagram of a 3-phase transformer and data given below.

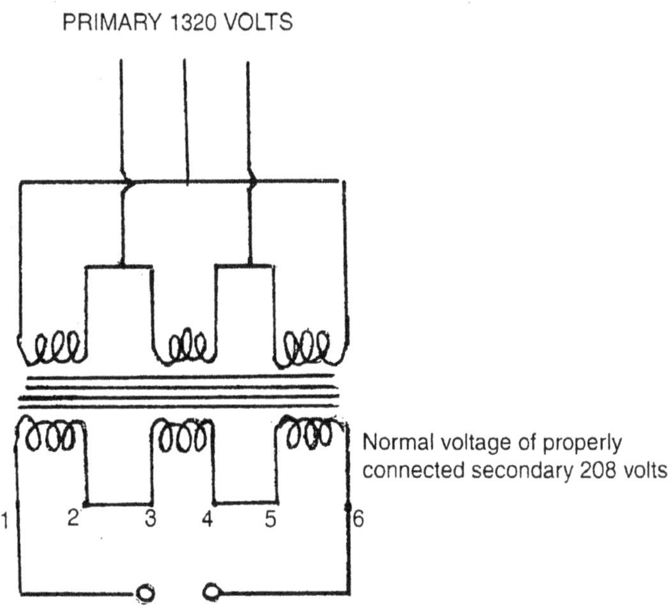


Data: The above transformer is to be connected delta-delta, with primary connections completed as shown. Assume that the connections of the secondary of the transformer bank are not completed and it is found that coil (1-2) is reversed. Under this condition:

10. The voltage between points 6 and 3 will be MOST NEARLY 10.____

   A. 208  B. 360  C. 416  D. 520

11. The voltage between points 1 and 6 will be MOST NEARLY 11.____

A. 208 B. 360 C. 416 D. 520

12. The voltage between points 1 and 4 will be MOST NEARLY 12.____

A. 208 B. 360 C. 416 D. 520

13. The one of the following types of valves which is GENERALLY used where extremely close regulation of flow is needed is the ______ valve. 13.____

A. gate B. glove C. needle D. blow-off

14. Lubricating oils of mineral origin are refined from ______ products. 14.____

A. lard-beef
B. cotton seed
C. crude petroleum
D. lime soap

Questions 15-17.

DIRECTIONS: Questions 15 through 17, inclusive, are to be answered in accordance with the diagram below.

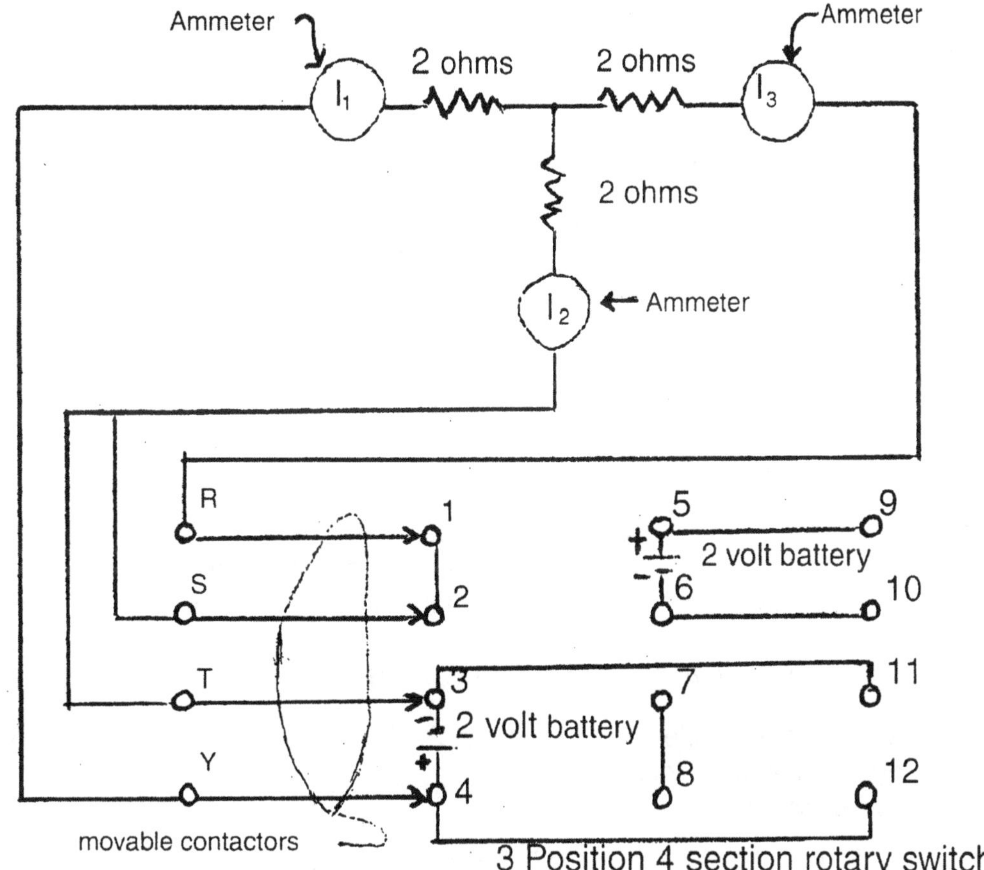


15. When switch movable contactors R, S, T, and V are in position 1, 2, 3, and 4, as shown, the current $I_1$, in amperes, is MOST NEARLY 15.____

A. 2 B. 2/3 C. 1/3 D. 1/6

16. When switch movable contactors R, S, T, and V are in position 5, 6, 7, and 8, the current $I_{2,}$ in amperes, is MOST NEARLY 16.____

A. 2 B. 2/3 C. 1/3 D. 1/6

17. When switch movable contactors R, S, T, and V are in position 9, 10, 11, and 12, the current, in amperes, registered by ammeter $I_3$ is MOST NEARLY 17.____

A. 3 B. 2 C. 2/3 D. 1/3

18. Light-bodied lubricating oils are MOST commonly used for 18.____

A. light loads at high speeds
B. heavy bearing pressure
C. heavy loads at slow speeds
D. chain drives and gears

19. The one of the following lubricants which is LEAST likely to be attacked by acids is 19.____

A. cottonseed oil
B. castor oil
C. rape seed oil
D. graphite

20. In general, non-rising stem gate valves are BEST adaptable for 20.____

A. use where frequent adjustments are necessary
B. installations carrying viscous liquids
C. throttling or close control
D. places where space is a factor

21. The presence of moisture in insulating oil is undesirable. The percentage of moisture which will reduce the dielectric strength of insulating oil to approximately one-half of its dielectric strength when dry is MOST NEARLY ______ of moisture. 21.____

A. 0.5% B. 0.05% C. 0.005% D. 0.0005%

22. It has been brought to your attention that one of the men under your supervision is complaining to fellow co-workers that another man has received an easy assignment through his *connections*. In this situation, it is BEST to 22.____

A. privately inform the man who is complaining of the truth regarding the assignment
B. in the presence of others, demand absolute proof from the man who is complaining
C. ignore the matter since it is not your job to interfere in disagreements between the men
D. tell the complaining man to apply for a desirable assignment also

23. In the standard method of testing electrical insulating oils, the test cup used to determine the dielectric strength contains two electrodes, each ______ inch in diameter with a gap of ______ inch between them. 23.____

A. 0.1; 1 B. 0.5; 0.3 C. 0.75; 0.3 D. 1.00; 0.1

24. The PROPER fire extinguishing agent to use to extinguish fires in electrical equipment is 24.____

A. water
B. foam
C. soda-acid
D. carbon dioxide

25. Circuit conductors operating at 600 volts or less may be worked upon live, without opening the circuit, if certain precautionary measures are taken. The one of the following that BEST represents one of these precautionary measures for this work is 25.____

A. bare or exposed places on one conductor must be taped after another conductor is first exposed
B. adjacent live or grounded conductor shall be covered with a conducting material
C. bare or exposed places on one conductor must be taped before another conductor is exposed
D. adjacent live or grounded conductors shall be securely bonded to ground

26. In order to properly distribute the load (in proportion to their rated capacities) between two alternators which are operating in parallel, it is necessary to 26.____

A. overexcite the smaller alternator and underexcite the larger one
B. adjust the governor on the prime mover
C. underexcite the larger alternator but use normal excitation on the smaller one
D. underexcite the smaller alternator and overexcite the larger one

27. If a large amount of flame is visible from a small pile of burning material, it is likely that the material MUST contain a substance that 27.____

A. contains a large amount of inorganic material
B. produces during the burning process a large amount of pure carbon
C. produces during the burning process a large amount of combustible gases or vapors
D. is composed almost entirely of pure carbon

28. If the velocity of water flow in a pipe is doubled, assuming other factors are constant, the loss of head due to friction will be 28.____

A. decreased 1/2 times B. decreased 1/4 times
C. increased 4 times D. the same

29. Reprimanding a subordinate for inefficiency in the presence of fellow co-workers is apt to 29.____

A. cause the subordinate to resign
B. arouse the subordinate's resentment
C. improve the performance of all present
D. cause the subordinate to improve

30. Assume that certain work assignments are not liked by any of your subordinates. Because this work has to be done, you, as the operator in charge, should try as much as possible to 30.____

A. assign this work as punishment details
B. rotate the work assignments among subordinates
C. assign this work to the best-natured man
D. assign this work to the junior men

31. A senior engineer, in discussing new departmental regulations with his subordinates, commented, *We should be conscious of the fact that our interests are mutual, and that by all of us in unison putting our shoulder to the wheel and working together, we can achieve our common objective.* This approach is 31.____

A. *good,* because this attitude will promote cooperation
B. *poor,* because this approach will invite excessive criticism
C. *good,* because it will promote good fellowship
D. *poor,* because this will invite too much familiarity

32. In the inspection of relays, the type of trouble generally encountered often depends on the type of relay. The one of the following which is NOT a trouble encountered with an induction-type relay is 32.____

A. friction between disc and magnet
B. dust on disc
C. foreign matter in the gear train
D. punctured bellows

33. With reference to diesel engines, the one of the following which is NOT a method of scavenging the cylinder is ______ scavenging. 33.____

A. crankcase
B. integral
C. under-piston
D. vane

34. Direct current motors for BEST performance should have their brushes set on the commutator 34.____

A. at the neutral point (under load)
B. at the point of maximum armature reaction
C. radially at an angle of 90 (leading)
D. radially at an angle of 80 (leading)

35. The PROPER order of events that take place in a 4-stroke cycle diesel engine is ______, and exhaust. 35.____

A. air intake, power expansion, compression
B. air intake, compression, power expansion
C. power expansion, air intake, compression
D. compression, air intake, power expansion

36. The compression ratio of a diesel engine that has no starting ignition device is GENERALLY in the range of 36.____

A. 11 to 20
B. 8 to 10
C. 6 to 8
D. 4 to 6

37. The base in a lubricating grease denotes the 37.____

A. type of soap that is used in its manufacture
B. consistency and the texture of the grease
C. dropping or melting point of the grease
D. carbon-residue content of the grease

38. Of the following sets of pipes, the one having a total combined area exactly equal to the area of a 12" diameter pipe is ______ pipes. 38.____

A. two 6"
B. two 8"
C. one 8" pipe and two 6"
D. four 6"

39. Assume that a single phase load takes EI x .8 watts, where E is the line voltage, I the line current, and .8 the power factor. The rating in volt-amperes of the synchronous condenser needed to raise the power factor to unity is MOST NEARLY EI x 39.____

A. .6 B. .8 C. .9 D. 1

40. If rubber gloves commonly used on high tension work are found on test to have pinholes, they 40.____

A. may be used on low voltage
B. should be discarded
C. should be patched with rubber tape
D. may be used only in dry places

---

## KEY (CORRECT ANSWERS)

| | | | |
|---|---|---|---|
| 1. D | 11. C | 21. C | 31. A |
| 2. C | 12. B | 22. A | 32. D |
| 3. B | 13. C | 23. D | 33. D |
| 4. D | 14. C | 24. D | 34. A |
| 5. A | 15. B | 25. C | 35. B |
| 6. A | 16. C | 26. B | 36. A |
| 7. A | 17. D | 27. C | 37. A |
| 8. C | 18. A | 28. C | 38. D |
| 9. D | 19. D | 29. B | 39. A |
| 10. A | 20. D | 30. B | 40. B |

---

# EXAMINATION SECTION
# TEST 1

DIRECTIONS: Answer the following questions directly, briefly, and succinctly.

1. How does the manner in which fuel and air are admitted to the cylinders of Diesel and gasoline engines differ?

2. In a Diesel engine, how is the heat required for ignition generated?

3. If a Diesel engine and a gasoline engine each have a compression ratio at the upper limit, which engine will develop the greater pressure during the compression event?

4. Why is energy from an external source necessary for ignition in a gasoline engine?

5. What is the relationship between the pressure in the cylinder after the compression event and the power output of an engine?

6. What determines the highest practical compression ratio for a gasoline engine?

7. List three factors which determine when ignition should occur.

8. Is maximum power developed in the cylinder of an engine before or after the piston reaches TDC?

9. Does the time required for combustion vary with engine speed?

10. Why is the pressure developed in the cylinder of a gasoline engine less when ignition occurs later than when it occurs at the normal ignition time?

11. How is fuel related to the maximum-combustion pressure developed in the cylinder of a Diesel engine?

12. With respect to Diesel engines, what is meant by turbulence?

13. Why is turbulence necessary in a cylinder of a Diesel engine?

14. Which *two* parts of a combustion space may include design features which aid in creating turbulence?

15. What is the principal constructional difference between an open combustion chamber and other types?

16. With respect to Diesel engines, what is precombustion?

17. Why is precombustion used in some engines?

18. In engines equipped with precombustion chambers, where is the major portion of the injected

19. Which characteristic of gasoline determines how much fuel will be vaporized?

20. What is meant by vapor lock?

21. In addition to difficulty in starting the engine, name two troubles which may occur if the gasoline is not completely vaporized when it enters the combustion space.

22. Name *two* symptoms of detonation which occur during engine operation.

23. With respect to the phases of combustion, when will detonation occur in a gasoline engine; in a Diesel engine?

24. In general, what causes detonation in a gasoline engine?

25. What is the principal factor which determines the octane rating of a fuel required for a given engine?

26. In a Diesel engine, what is meant by ignition delay?

27. In addition to the characteristics of the fuel, which factors determine the duration of ignition delay in a Diesel engine?

28. Are fuels with a low or high volatility most desirable for Diesel engines?

---

# CORRECT ANSWERS

1. Fuel and air are admitted separately to the cylinders of a Diesel engine; and as a mixture to the cylinders of a gasoline engine.
2. By compression of intake air.
3. Diesel.
4. Because the heat caused by compression is not great enough to cause self-ignition of the combustible mixture.
5. The higher the pressure, the greater the power output.
6. The characteristics of the fuel used.
7. Engine speed, type of fuel, and compression ratio.
8. After.
9. No.
10. Because combustion takes place in larger space.
11. The rate and amount of fuel injected determine maximum pressure.
12. Motion of air within the combustion space.
13. To bring sufficient air in contact with injected fuel particles to ensure complete combustion.
14. Piston crown and cylinder head.
15. Open chambers have no auxiliary combustion chambers.
16. The conditioning of all or part of the fuel, by partial burning, before it enters the main combustion space.
17. To aid in creating the turbulence necessary for the proper mixing of air and fuel.
18. Main combustion space.
19. Volatility.
20. The formation of vapors in the fuel system which block or restrict the flow of fuel to the carburetor.
21. Improper fuel distribution and crankcase dilution.
22. Loss of power and undesirable, combustion noises.
23. During the final phase; start of second phase.
24. Anything which increases excessively the temperature or pressure of the unburned mixture in the combustion space.

25. Compression ratio.

26. The interval of time between the injection and the ignition of fuel.

27. The temperature and pressure of the compressed air in the combustion space, the average size of the injected
28. fuel particles and the amount of turbulence in the combustion space.

29. Fuels with a low volatility.

---

# TEST 2

DIRECTIONS: Answer the following questions directly, briefly, and succinctly.

1. What is the *BASIC* difference between the two common types of spark-ignition systems?
2. What is the *PRIMARY* purpose of the battery in a spark-ignition system?
3. What is the purpose of the shell of laminated iron that usually encloses the windings of an ignition coil?
4. What is the *BASIS* for sometimes calling the ignition coil of a battery-ignition system an induction coil?
5. What is the *PURPOSE* of the breaker assembly in an ignition system?
6. In what *two* ways may the two-coil, double-breaker assembly arrangement be used in an ignition system?
7. What happens to the voltage in the primary circuit of an ignition system when a high voltage is induced in the secondary winding of an ignition coil?
8. Which part of an ignition system functions to prevent arcing across the breaker-assembly points as they open?
9. What are the two *PRINCIPAL* parts of an ignition system distributing mechanism?
10. What is the *FUNCTION* of the rotating part of a distributing mechanism?
11. Why are the distributor rotor and the breaker-assembly cam driven at-one-half engine speed?
12. What causes the points of a breaker assembly to open and close?
13. If the breaker assembly is moved a few degrees in a direction opposite to the direction of cam rotation, is the time of spark occurrence, with respect to piston position, retarded or advanced?
14. If the time of spark occurrence is changed by moving the breaker-assembly cam, will moving the cam in a direction opposite to the direction of rotation retard or advance the spark?
15. Which forces are utilized to operate automatic spark-control devices so that the time of spark is advanced?
16. When engine speed decreases, what causes an automatic spark-control mechanism to retard the spark?
17. Which type of automatic control mechanism is used when variations in the timing of the spark are governed by engine speed?
18. Why are centrifugal and vacuum-type spark-control mechanisms sometimes used in combination?
19. The force which causes a distributor to move from the retarded position is transmitted from which part in a vacuum spark-control mechanism?

20. When a vacuum spark-control mechanism is in the retarded position, will the opening of the passage to the control unit be on the carburetor side or the manifold side of the throttle valve?

21. What is the *PRINCIPAL* difference between the two common types of spark plugs?

22. What determines the extent to which a spark plug will dissipate heat?

23. How do the metal housings or braided metal casings sometimes used to enclose the components of an ignition system prevent electrical interference in radio receiving equipment?

24. On the basis of the manner in which electromagnetic induction may be produced in a magneto, what are the two types of magnetos?

25. Is a separate ignition coil *NECESSARY* with a magneto which generates high voltage?

26. Is the distributing mechanism of a low-voltage magneto-ignition system located in the primary circuit or in the secondary circuit?

27. With respect to circuits, how does the location of the distributing mechanism in a low-voltage magneto-ignition *system differ* from the location of this mechanism in other types of ignition systems?

28. List *three* advantages which a low-voltage magneto-ignition system has over a magneto system of the high-voltage type?

29. If a magneto does not generate the high voltage required for ignition when an engine is being started, how is the necessary voltage obtained during the cranking interval?

30. Does the current from the booster coil flow through the magneto?

31. What is the difference in the manner by which ignition-over-speed safety devices function to control speed in battery-ignition and magneto-ignition systems?

---

# CORRECT ANSWERS

1. The source of electrical energy.
2. To energize the secondary, or high-voltage, winding of the ignition coil.
3. To serve as a conductor for the magnetic field.
4. The coil operates on the principle of electromagnetic induction; in other words, the coil depends on the inductive effect of the magnetism produced by the low voltage in the primary winding to produce high voltage in the secondary winding.
5. To act as a switch, opening and closing the primary circuit.
6. To provide a single spark to each cylinder; and to provide two sparks simultaneously to each cylinder.
7. It is momentarily increased because a voltage is also induced in the primary circuit when the breaker points open and the magnetic field collapses.
8. The condenser.
9. Rotor (distributing arm) and cap (head).
10. To close the secondary circuit, so that current from a high-voltage side of the coil will flow to the proper spark plug.
11. So that half of the spark plugs will fire during each revolution of the crankshaft.
12. Lobes on the breaker-assembly cam.
13. Advanced.
14. Retard.
15. Centrifugal force and vacuum.
16. The action of springs.
17. Centrifugal.
18. So that proper spark-control is provided under all conditions of speed and load.
19. Spring-loaded diaphragm.
20. On the carburetor side.
21. The material used in the insulator or core.
22. The amount of insulator exposed to the combustion gases.
23. By absorbing and grounding the high-frequency current given off by the parts of the ignition system.

24. Armature wound and inductor type.

25. No.

26. In the primary circuit.

27. In the low-voltage magneto system, the distributing mechanism is located in the primary circuit; and it is located in the secondary circuit in the battery-ignition and high-voltage magneto-ignition systems.

28. Shorter high-voltage leads, less electrical loss, and problems of a less serious nature in insulation and shielding.

29. Either from a booster coil-and-battery circuit or from the magneto by increasing its speed with an impulse mechanism.

30. No.

31. In a battery ignition system, the safety device opens the primary circuit to stop the flow of current; in a magneto-ignition system, the primary circuit is grounded.

---

# TEST 3

DIRECTIONS: Answer the following questions directly, briefly, and succinctly.

1. Name *four* functions of an engine lubricating oil.
2. How does lubricating oil reduce friction between bearing surfaces?
3. In addition to reducing friction, why is an oil seal necessary between the piston rings and the cylinder wall?
4. What are the PRINCIPAL engine parts which lubricating, oil may cool?
5. With respect to the engine, where may the heat absorbed by lubricating oil be dissipated?
6. The thickness of the oil film between two bearing surfaces is determined *PRINCIPALLY* by which property of the oil?
7. Which characteristics of an engine determine the viscosity of the lubricating Oil to be used?
8. What is meant by the detergent power of an oil?
9. What is the purpose of the symbol numbers assigned to oils?
10. How are the lubricating qualities of an oil *IMPROVED* by chemical additives?
11. If the recommended compounded oil is not available in sufficient quantities, would it be *better* to use a straight mineral oil or a mixture of additive- and mineral-type oils?
12. What is the *most likely* source of trouble if corrosion is found on the internal surfaces of an engine which uses compounded oil?
13. Does the suspension of fine particles of gummy material and carbon in an additive-type oil indicate a reduction in the lubricating quality of the oil?
14. In a centrifugal purifier, what causes sediment, water, and oil to form separate layers?
15. In brief, what is the purification process when a purifier is used as a separator? As a clarifier?
16. What determines whether a purifier should be used as a separator or as a clarifier?
17. Is the principle of operation or the design of the rotating elements the *principal* difference between the two common types of purifiers?
18. In which type of purifier does the oil enter and leave through the top of the bowl?
19. What is the purpose of the three-wing device in the bowl of a tubular type purifier?
20. When should a purifier be operated at tees than rated capacity?
21. When a purifier is used as a separator, what will be the result if the bowl is *NOT* primed with water?
22. What is the *PRINCIPAL* factor determining the length of time required to purify a lubricating oil?

23. Should the pressure or the temperature of the oil admitted to a purifier be increased in order to facilitate purification?

24. What is the result if the pressure on the oil admitted to a purifier is reduced? *Why*

25. What determines the size of the discharge ring to be used for the purification of a given oil?

26. How can the general efficiency of a purifier be determined if an analysis of the purified oil Cannot be made?

27. What type of chemical compound is included in a grease which is to be used where operating temperatures and loads are not excessive but where moisture is present?

28. Why is graphite grease *NOT* recommended as a lubricant for ball bearings or roller bearings?

---

# CORRECT ANSWERS

1. To prevent metal-to-metal contact; to form a seal between the piston rings and the cylinder; to aid in engine cooling; and to aid in preventing and removing sludge formations.

2. By forming a film which prevents direct contact between moving metal surfaces.

3. To prevent blow-by of gases.

4. Bearings, journals, and pistons.

5. To the mass of oil in the sump or to the water in the cooling system.

6. Viscosity.

7. Operating temperatures, speeds, pressures, and bearing clearances.

8. The oil's ability to remove or to prevent the accumulation of carbon deposits.

9. To identify the use and viscosity of each oil.

10. The tendency of the oil to stick to metal surfaces and the natural detergent property of the oil are improved by additives; additives also inhibit oxidation.

11. A mixture of additive- and mineral-type oils.

12. Water or partially burned fuel in the lubricating oil.

13. No.

14. The difference in the specific gravities of the sediment, water, and oil.

15. When used as a separator, the purifier separates oil from water and sediment. When used as a clarifier, a purifier separates oil from sediment only.

16. The moisture content of the oil being purified.

17. The design of the rotating elements.

18. Disk type.

19. To rotate the oil at the speed at which the bowl is rotating.

20. When it is being used as a separator with 9000 series oil.

21. Oil will be lost though the water-discharge ports.

22. The viscosity of the oil.

23. Temperature.

24. Purification is improved, because the reduction in the pressure increases the length of time the oil is subjected to centrifugal force.

25. The specific gravity of the oil.

26. By observing the clarity of the purified oil and the amount of oil in the separated water.

27. A lime-soap.

28. Because of its abrasive characteristic.

---

# TEST 4

DIRECTIONS: Answer the following questions directly, briefly, and succinctly.

1. Which type of pump is used in engine lubricating-oil systems?
2. Name *two* types of pressure-control devices that may be incorporated in a lubricating-oil pump.
3. How does a control device regulate lubricating-oil pressure?
4. Why are *two* elements included in some lubricating-oil strainers?
5. Is oil flow to the engine stopped when a simplex strainer becomes clogged? *Why*?
6. Name *two* types of elements that are used in metal-edge type strainers.
7. How is the element of a metal-edge type strainer cleaned, without connections being broken or the flow of oil being interrupted?
8. Screen-type strainers are usually located on which side of the pressure pump?
9. Why is Fuller's earth *NOT* permitted in filters approved for use in engine lubricating-oil systems?
10. Name *three* types of lubricating-oil filtering systems.
11. In which type of lubricating-oil filtering system does all of the oil discharged by the pump flow directly to the engine through a strainer, a filter, and a cooler?
12. How does a sump-type filtering system *differ from* a shunt-type system?
13. With which type lubricating-oil-filtering system is it possible to filter the oil when the engine is not operating?
14. In a lubricating-oil system in which the filtering system is of the sump type, what is the path of oil from the oil supply to the engine inlet? (Indicate path by listing main components in the proper order.)
15. Name the two types of filtering systems in which oil flows directly from the filter back to the sump.
16. What *LIMITS* the amount of oil which flows through the filter of a bypass-type filtering system?
17. By listing the main parts of the system in their proper order, trace the path of oil through the external section of a lubricating-oil system which includes a shunt-type filtering system.
18. Name two ways in which oil for cooling may be supplied to the pistons of an engine.
19. What is the *FIRST* part to which lubricating oil usually flows after it enters the engine?
20. When is use made of the auxiliary pump which is incorporated in some lubricating systems?
21. How is oil supplied to the crankpin bearings, in most engines?
22. How are the crankshaft bearings lubricated in small gasoline engines which have no lubricating oil system?

23. List four *UNDESIRABLE* conditions which may occur if the crankcase of an engine is not properly ventilated.

24. In gasoline engines, unburned fuel may blow-by the compression rings, enter the crankcase, and dilute the lubricating oil. This situation is less likely to occur in a 2-stroke cycle engine. *Why*?

25. How are oil particles sometimes prevented from entering the blowers of engines in which the crankcase is ventilated to the intake system?

26. What happens to the harmful vapors which are vented from the crankcase to the intake system?

27. How may a crankshaft-bearing failure lead to a crankcase explosion?

28. What is the BEST source of information when you are checking an operating engine for symptoms of an impending bearing failure?

29. Why will fuel-diluted lubricating oil contribute *more readily* to conditions which may cause a crankcase explosion, than will oil which is not diluted by fuel?

---

# CORRECT ANSWERS

1. Positive-displacement rotary-gear pump.

2. Pressure-regulating valve; pressure-relief valve.

3. By recirculating excess oil from the pump discharge back to the pump intake or by discharging the excess oil directly to the oil sump.

4. In order that one element can be bypassed and removed for cleaning without interruption to the flow of oil to the engine.

5. No, because strainers of this type are provided with pressure-relief valves through which all oil may be bypassed to the engine.

6. Edge-wound metal ribbon; edge-type disks.

7. By manual rotation of the element against metallic scrapers, which remove the material caught by the element.

8. On the suction, or intake, side.

9. Fuller's earth removes the compounds (detergents) from additive-type oils.

10. Shunt, sump, and bypass.

11. Shunt.

12. In a sump-type filtering system, the filter is placed in a separate system in which oil is circulated by a motor-driven pump; the filter in a shunt-type system is located in the main lubricating-oil system.

13. Sump-type filtering system.

14. Sump, pump, cooler, and strainer.

15. Sump-type and bypass-type.

16. The size of the piping, and an orifice.

17. Sump tank, pump, strainer, filter, and cooler.

18. (a) Through drilled passages in the connecting rod.
    (b) By nozzles connected to an oil manifold.

19. Manifold (also called galley, or header).

20. An auxiliary pump is used if the lubricating-oil pump fails; it may also be used to circulate oil through the system when the engine is not operating.

21. Crankpin bearings usually receive oil from the main bearings, through drilled passages in the crankshaft.

22. By oil, mixed with the gasoline, which enters the engine with the fuel-air mixture.

23. An explosive mixture may accumulate; the lubricating oil may be diluted; corrosion may take place within the crankcase; and the lubricating oil may become emulsified.

24. Because the unburned fuel which might blow-by the compression rings is trapped in the intake ports and is forced back into the combustion space by the scavenging air when the intake ports are uncovered by the piston.

25. By the fine-wire screen device which separates the oil from the ventilating air and causes the oil to drain back to the oil supply.

26. They are forced into the combustion space and are either burned or discharged with the exhaust.

27. By causing excess heat, which vaporizes the oil; and by causing sparks, which may ignite the explosive mixture.

28. The oil pressure gage.

29. Because the flash point of the fuel is lower than that of lubricating oil, fuel-diluted oil tends to form an explosive mixture more rapidly than does lubricating oil, which is not diluted.

---

# TEST 5

DIRECTIONS: Answer the following questions directly, briefly, and succinctly.

1. List *three* reasons why the temperature of an engine MUST NOT be allowed to exceed a specified limit.
2. How may excessive heat in an engine affect lubrication?
3. How may too low an engine temperature affect the lubricating oil and the cylinders of an engine?
4. How may inadequate engine cooling cause a wrist pin to seize?
5. Trace the path which water follows in a typical open cooling system, by listing the various parts and passages in the proper order.
6. Does the water flow through the exhaust-silencer water jacket after passing through the engine in all open cooling systems?
7. In engines equipped with open cooling systems, what are two possible sources of the heat that is used to raise the temperature of engine intake water?
8. In a closed cooling system, how is salt-water cooling of the fresh water accomplished if there is no separate sea-water circuit?
9. Starting with the discharge side of the fresh-water pump, trace the path of water through the fresh-water circuit of a cooling system by listing the parts and passages in the proper order.
10. Trace the path of water through the sea-water circuit of a closed cooling system by listing the parts and passages in the proper order.
11. Why is an auxiliary, or detached, pump provided in the cooling systems of some engines?
12. Name *three* ways in which the fresh- and sea-water pumps of a cooling system may differ.
13. Name *three* types of pumps which are used in engine cooling systems.
14. Of the three types of pumps used in engine cooling systems, which is the *most common*?
15. Name *three* methods by which tee pumps of a cooling system may be driven.
16. Name *three* fluids, essential to engine operation, the temperatures of which are maintained at proper operating levels by coolers.
17. Coolers, as used in the cooling systems of engines, may be of which *three* types?
18. Name the two *PRINCIPAL* parts of a shell-and-tube cooler.
19. Describe briefly the paths which the cooling and cooled liquids generally take through a shell-and-tube cooler.
20. In a shell-and-tube cooler, why is one of the tube sheets so arranged that it "floats" within the shell?
21. What is meant by the term *counterflow* when it is used to describe a type of shell-and-tube cooler?

22. Is a strut-tube cooler *larger* or *smaller* than a shell-and-tube cooler which provides the same amount of heat transfer?

23. If a strut-tube cooler and a shell-and-tube cooler provide an equal amount of heat transfer, which will withstand a HIGHER degree of scaling and larger foreign particles without clogging the cooling system?

24. Name *three* functions served by the "struts" in a strut-tube water cooler.

25. Of the three types of coolers used in engine cooling systems, which one is used *only* for the cooling of lubricating oil?

26. What is a "hull" cooler?

27. Which devices are installed in the salt-water circuit of an engine cooling system to protect the circuit from corrosion caused by electrolysis?

28. Do the devices which are installed to protect the sea-water circuit from corrosion prevent galvanic action?

29. Which terms are used to distinguish between the forms, or types, of zincs?

30. Which of the engine cooling passages which are common to in-line and V-type engines are not found in engines of the opposed-piston type?

31. Indicate how the paths of water through the GM 16-278A and FM 38D differ, by listing, in the order of flow, the parts and passages for each engine (start and end with the pump).

32. What is the *PURPOSE* of the tank that is provided in the freshwater circuit of an engine cooling system?

---

# CORRECT ANSWERS

1. To maintain adequate lubrication; to prevent excessive variations in dimensions of parts; and to retain strength of metals.

2. Excess heat may reduce viscosity to a point where the oil film between parts may be destroyed. Also, heat causes oxidation of the oil and the formation of sludge.

3. An excessively low engine temperature may: cause corrosive gases to condense on the cylinder walls; increase ignition lag, causing detonation; and cause condensation, which leads to the formation of acid and sludge in the lubricating oil.

4. Inadequate cooling may allow an engine to overheat to the extent that closely fitted parts will seize because of the expansion of parts and the reduction of clearance.

5. Sea chest or scoop, strainer, sea valves, pump, lubricating-oil cooler, engine passages and jackets, exhaust-silencer water jackets, and overboard outlet.

6. No.

7. Lubricating oil and exhaust gases.

8. The fresh-water cooler is located outside of the hull, below the water line, in direct contact with the sea water.

9. Pump (discharge), engine passages, fresh-water cooler, lubricating-oil cooler (when applicable), and pump (suction).

10. Sea chest, strainer, sea valves, fresh-water cooler, lubricating-oil cooler (when applicable), exhaust cooling passages, and overboard outlets.

11. To be used in the event of attached-pump failure and to provide a means of cooling after the engine has been secured.

12. Fresh- and sea-water pumps may differ in type, size, and capacity.

13. Centrifugal, gear, and rotary (vane).

14. Centrifugal.

15. Gears, pulley and V-belt, and coupling.

16. Fresh water, lubricating, oil, and air (in some cases).

17. Shell-and-tube, strut-tube, and plate-tube.

18. The tube bundle (bank, nest) and the shell.

19. The cooled liquid generally flows through the tubes; the cooling liquid generally flows around the tubes.

20. To allow for expansion of the tube bundle.

21. That the direction of liquid flow in the tubes is opposite to that in the shell.

22. Smaller.

23. The shell-and-tube cooler.

24. "Struts" increase the inside and outside contact surfaces of the tube, create turbulence in the liquid flowing through the tube, and increase the structural strength of the tube.

25. Plate-tube cooler.

26. A fresh-water cooler which is located outside the hull, below the water line, in direct contact with the sea water.

27. Zincs.

28. No. Zincs are installed to provide a replaceable surface for the attach of galvanic action.

29. Pencil and plate.

30. Cylinder-head passages.

31. GM 16-278A: Pump, water manifold, liner passages, head passages, exhaust passages, cooler, and pump. FM 38D: Pump, exhaust passages, liner passages, water header, cooler, pump.

32. The tank provides a place where water may be added to the system, and a space to accommodate variations in the volume of the water.

---

# BASIC FUNDAMENTALS OF ELECTRICITY

## CONTENTS



---

# BASIC FUNDAMENTALS OF ELECTRICITY

## Electricity

### Unit 1

When you use a small hand drill, the energy that turns the drill comes from your body. When you snap the switch on an electric drill, another form of energy spins the bit of the drill. We call this form of energy *electricity.* Electrical energy plays a vital part in our environment. It lights our houses, cooks our food, runs our factories, and carries messages for us.

Like other forms of energy, electricity is something that we cannot create. We get it by converting another form of energy into electrical energy. The energy in running water is often used to produce, or *generate,* electricity. Waterpower can be used to turn a generator, which converts the energy in running water into electrical energy. Plants which use this process are called *hydroelectric* plants.

In the United States most of our electricity is produced by changing heat energy into electrical energy. A plant which uses this process is called a thermoelectric plant. In a *thermoelectric* plant, heat energy is first changed into mechanical energy. A steam turbine is often used for this purpose. Then the mechanical energy, produced by the turbine, is changed into electrical energy by a large *generator.* Today we produce some electricity also by changing atomic energy into electric energy.

***Electrical Charges***

Electricity is a form of energy produced when an electrical charge moves along a wire. Let us try to explain what an electrical charge is. If you lift a brick into the air, the brick acquires potential energy. You have separated the brick from the ground by using energy in your body. If you drop the brick, it will move to the ground, expending the energy it picked up when it was lifted. If the brick strikes a pane of glass on the way down, the energy in the brick will break the glass. The moving brick has kinetic energy; it will do work.

Electricity depends on this same principle. Inside the atom the tiny particles called *protons and electrons* are attracted to one another just as the brick is attracted to the ground. The proton and electron are called *charged particles.* The proton carries a *positive* charge. The electron carries a *negative* charge. They attract one another. If we force them apart, we must use energy, just as we use energy to raise a brick. When we release them, the electrons and protons move back together. While they are moving they can do work. For convenience sake, we say that the electrons move toward the protons.

Whenever electrons are moving, electricity is present. As they move, electrons can do work. They have energy. The reason they have energy is the same as the reason the brick has energy. Work must be done to separate electrons and protons. When they come back together, the energy they picked up is released.

***Eletrical Energy***

Let's take a simple example. Suppose we have a small heap of protons and electrons. We take all the electrons in one hand, and all the protons in the other hand. Then we pull them apart. Since they attract each other, we must use energy when we pull them apart. The electrons and protons then have potential energy. If they can, they will move back together again.

If we connect the two piles with a wire, the electrons will move along the wire and return to the protons. Like the falling brick, the electrons have energy as they move back to the protons. If we put a glass pane under the brick, we can make the brick use some of its energy to break the glass.

If we put a hurdle in front of the electrons, we can make them work as they move back toward the protons. That is the basis of all electricity-powered equipment. Electrons are made to use some of their energy as they try to return to the protons.

Suppose we connect electrons and protons by a wire, but we put in a high hurdle that the electrons must cross. As the electrons move over the hurdle, they release some of their energy. The electron must use energy to jump the hurdle just as we do. This energy is not destroyed. It is converted into heat. A "hot spot" will appear in the wire at the hurdle we placed in the road. If we put the resistance inside a glass bulb, and take out most of the air, the spot will glow white. We will have made an electric light bulb. By making the electrons work as they returned to the protons, we have created a light that we can use.

### *Electron flow*

This illustration is a little too simple. But all electricity works on this general principle. Actually, one electron usually does not move the whole length of a wire. It moves only a short distance. The effect is like one billiard ball striking a long row of billiard balls. The shock is passed from one ball to the next, but each ball does not move very far. Another example is the way a shock runs through a long train when the engine stops. In any electric wire there are millions and millions of electrons that pass the movement along. This is called electron flow. The flow of electrons is the form of energy we call electricity.

The flow of electrons along a wire depends upon the way electrons are placed in an atom. You remember that electrons are arranged in shells around the nucleus of the atom. The nucleus has a positive charge. The electrons have a negative charge. In some atoms the electrons in the outer shell can be knocked loose very easily. Loose electrons are called *free electrons,* and they are the carriers of electrical energy. When the wire connects a supply of protons and a supply of electrons, these free electrons move along the wire-or drift-toward the protons. This movement produces an *electric current.*

### *Conductors and Insulators*

If there are no free electrons, no electric current can be produced. Some materials produce hirge numbers of free electrons. They can carry an electric current very easily. These materials are called *conductors* because they conduct electricity. Other materials contain few free electrons. Little or, no electricity can flow through them. They are called *insulators.* They do not conduct electricity. Materials like silver, copper, aluminum, and gold possess many free electrons. They are good electrical conductors. Because copper is inexpensive, it is used most often for electrical wire. Materials like glass, rubber, wood, air, and paper are *insulators.* They do not carry electricity because they have few free electrons.

### *Measuring Electricity*

When electrons flow along a conductor, we have electrical energy. Energy passes along the wire at the same speed as light, 186,000 miles each second. But how much electrical energy is passing through the wire? How much work can the electricity do? To answer these questions, we must measure electricity. To measure, we must have standards.

To find out how much electricity we have, we need only count the number of electrons available. If there are 6¼ billion billion electrons separated from protons, we have one *coulomb* of electrical charge. This sounds like a large number of electrons. But it is only a small amount of electricity.

A second question we must answer is, "How hard are the electrons trying to get back to the protons? How much pressure do they exert?" If we have electrons in one hand and protons in the other, how hard do they pull? The standard unit used by science to measure electrical pressure is based on the coulomb. If one coulomb of electrons is available, the amount of pressure they produce is defined as one *volt.* This is our standard for electrical pressure. If we have five coulombs of electrons in one hand, they will exert five volts of pressure trying to return to the protons. The volt is often called an *electromotive* force, and abbreviated as *emf*, or just a capital *E*. In our formulas, we will always abbreviate volts as *E*.

The coulomb and the volt measure potential energy. They tell us how many electrons we are holding. This is like weighing a rock we have lifted off the ground. But we would also like to know about electricity when it is in action. How fast are the electrons moving in our wire? To find this, we simply measure the number of electrons that pass one point in one second. If one coulomb of electrons flows past in one second, we say that one *ampere* of electric current is flowing in the wire. In other words, if one coulomb of electronsmoves past a point in one second, one ampere of electricity is flowing.

Notice that all of these definitions are tied together. One coulomb is equal to 6¼ billion billion electrons. This number of electrons produces one volt of pressure. If one coulomb of electrons flows each second, the current is called one ampere. Of course, electricity will flow only when two points are connected. It will flow only if there is some separation of electrons and protons. If the number of electrons and the number of protons are equal at the same ends of a wire, no electricity will flow.

***Resistance***

When you apply energy to a machine like the wheel and axle, you lose some of the energy inside the machine because of friction. If you apply electrical energy to a wire, you also lose some energy in the wire. This loss is due to the *resistance* of the wire. The wire must have free electrons to carry electrical energy through the wire. But the electrons are tied to the nucleus of the atom by a small force. This force must be overcome before the electrons are free. The energy to free the electrons must be supplied from the energy in the electrons moving into the wire.

In a machine we must know how much energy we lose to friction to know the efficiency of the machine. We also measure the amount of loss in an electrical conductor. To do this, we measure the resistance of the conductor. Now, we know that the energy lost was used to pull electrons loose from their shells. And we know that this energy is converted into heat. So if we measure the amount of heat generated in a conductor, we know how much energy we have lost.

The standard unit used to measure resistance is called the ohm. This is the amount of resistance that generates 0.24 calories of heat when one ampere of electrical current flows through a wire. In other words, we run one ampere of current through a wire and measure the heat that is produced. If the heat equals 0.24 calories, then the resistance of the wire is one ohm. This definition of the unit of resistance ties it to all the other measuring standards in electricity. Look at the following table.

| NAME OF UNIT | MEANING | UNINT | ABBREVIATION |
|---|---|---|---|
| Voltage | Pressure, or potential difference | Volt | *E* |
| Current | Flow of Electrons | Ampere | *I* |
| Resistance | Opposition to the flow of electrons | Ohm | *R* |

***Ohm's Law***

If we separate electrons and protons and keep them separated, we have a potential difference between them. If we connect these two points with a conductor, we have an *electrical circuit*. When the two points are connected, electrons will flow through the conductor. We can find the voltage, the current, and the resistance in any electrical circuit by using a simple formula called *Ohm's Law*. This is one of the basic laws in all electricity, and you should learn it thoroughly. Ohm said that in any electrical circuit:

1. The current flowing is equal to the voltage divided by the resistance.
2. The resistance is equal to the voltage divided by the current.

3. The voltage is equal to the resistance multiplied by the current.

These three rules apply simply because they are defined that way. We know that one volt of electricity will push one ampere of current across a resistance of one ohm. Ohm produced his three rules by combining the definitions into one general rule. The formula is:

$$\text{Current}(I)\frac{(E)\text{voltage}}{(R)\text{ resistance}}$$

We can write this in three ways:

1. $I = \frac{E}{R}$ 2. $E = I \times R$ 3. $R\frac{E}{R}$

Learn all three forms of Ohm's Law thoroughly.

***Using Ohm's Law***

In the United States most of our houses are wired for 110 volts of electricity. Suppose you had a heater that had a resistance of eleven ohms. But you did not know how many amperes of current the heater used. Ohm's Law could tell you the answer easily. You know the voltage and resistance. You want to know the current. Using formula 1 above:

$$I = \frac{E}{R} \qquad I = \frac{110}{11} \qquad I = 10 \text{ amperes}$$

Your heater would need a ten ampere fuse. You can solve any other problems of this type using the same formula.

**Power**

If we know the voltage, current, and resistance in an electrical current, we still do not know how much energy the circuit is using. This can be a serious problem when we want to figure out our own electricity bills.

The unit of electrical power is the watt. This is the amount of work done in one second when one volt of electricity moves one ampere of current through a circuit. In other words, if we have one volt of pressure and it moves one ampere of current through the circuit, we are using one watt of electrical energy. When larger units are needed, we use the unit called the kilowatt which is equal to one thousand watts.

To find the power (in watts) used in a circuit, simply multiply the voltage of the circuit by the current flowing through a circuit. The power formula is written:

Power ($W$) = ($E$) Voltage X ($I$) Current

Almost every electrical problem can be solved by using the power formula, or combining the power formula with Ohm's Law.

*Examples*

1. An air conditioner has a tag which states that the unit uses 2,200 watts of power. The unit plugs into 110 volt electricity. How large must the fuse be in the line?

a. $W = E \times I$ or $2{,}200 = 110 \times I$

b. $I = \frac{2{,}200}{110}$ or $I = 20$ ampers

The air conditioner will use a twenty ampere fuse. This is a very heavy load for house wiring, and the wiring should be checked before adding this much current to a line.

2. You have just bought a new electric heater. It operates on 110 volt electricity, and it has a resistance of ten ohms. You pay five cents for each kilowatt of electricity. How much will it cost to run the heater for thirty days?

a. First, you must use Ohm's Law to find the current that flows through the heater:

$$I=\frac{E}{R} \qquad I=\frac{110}{10} \qquad I=11 \text{ amperes}$$

b. Then you find the number of watts the heater uses, using the power formula:

$$W=E \times I \qquad W=110 \times 11 \qquad W=1{,}210 \text{ watts}$$

c. Now you know that the heater uses 1.21 kilowatts every hour. This electricity costs five cents for each kilowatt hour. You can figure that the heater will cost about six cents per hour to run. If it ran day and night for thirty days, the total cost would be approximately forty-three dollars ($43.56, to be exact). This is the way you can use the two formulas to work out electrical problems in the home.

**Words Used in Unit 1**

**abbreviated** (ə brē´vĭ āt əd), shortened
**convenience** (kən vēn´ yəns), saving of trouble
**electron** (ĭ lĕk´trŏn), a tiny particle carrying one unit of negative electricity
**expending** (ĕks pĕnd´ĭng), i using up
**hurdle** (hər´ dəl), an obstacle in one's way
**illustration** (ĭl əs trā´shən ), story, example
**proton** (prō´tŏn), tiny particle carrying one unit of positive electricity
**thermoelectric** (thər mō ĭ lĕk´trĭk), having to do with electricity produced by heat

# Magnetism

## Unit 2

If you take a small piece of the mineral magnetite and hold it near some iron filings, the iron filings will cling to the magnetite. This material is called a *natural magnet.* Since this magnet actually pulls the iron filings toward it, we know that it can do work. So we know that a magnet contains energy of some sort.

We can make a magnet with electricity, too. If we wrap some wire around an iron spike and run an electric current through the wire, the spike will also attract iron filings. But the spike will attract iron onlv while the electric current is flowing. When the current is shut off, the spike loses its magnetism. Such a magnet is called an electromagnet.

What is this mysterious force that draws the iron to the magnet? We know that it is related to electricity because we can produce magnetism by electricity.

### *What's a Magnet?*

Like most basic questions about our universe, this isa hard question to answer. We know that the molecules inside a magnet are organized. They are so arranged that there is potential difference between the two ends of the magnet. That is, one end has a positive charge and the other end has a negative charge. We know that energy must have been used to make this arrangement. Each end of the magnet is called a pole. We say that one pole is positive and the other is negative. The two poles act like electrons and protons. That is, likes repel each other; opposites attract. Two positive poles repel each other, and two negative poles repel each other. But a positive· pole and a negative pole will attract one another.

The charges at the poles of a magnet are probably due to the movement of electrons inside the magnet. We are not exactly certain what bring this about. But we do know a great deal about the way magnets work. And we know many of the relations between magnetism and electricity. These are the things we will study in this unit.

### *Magnetic fields*

A magnet attracts an iron filing *before* it touches the filing. The area around a magnet is charged, and the charge around the magnet pulls the iron toward the magnet. This charged area is called a magnetic field. Without these magnetic fields there could be no electricity as we know it.

The magnetic field increases in strength as we move closer to the surface of the magnet. If we place a magnet beneath a sheet of paper, and sprinkle tiny iron particles on the paper, the iron particles will arrange themselves along field lines of the magnet. Notice the pattern the lines form. Near the poles the lines are close together. The field is very strong here. At the center point between the poles, the lines are spread apart. The field is weakest here.

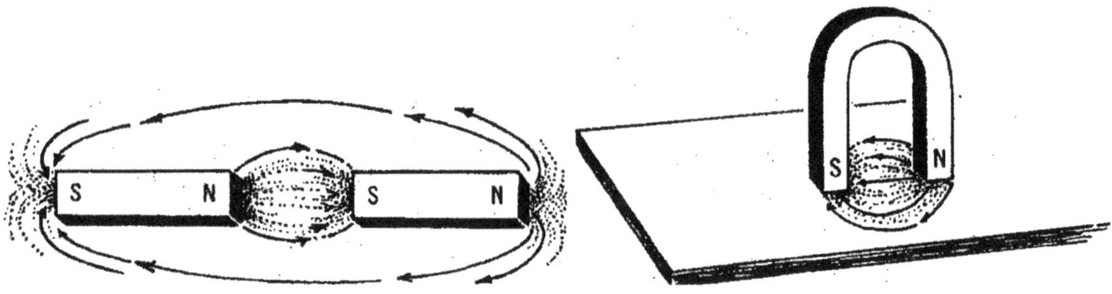


Fig. 1 a

Fig. 1 b

Figures 1a, 1 b Magnetic Lines of Force-Bar Magnet and Horseshoe Magnet.

The strength of the magnet determines the strength of the field. If we place a pieee of iron in the field, it concentrates the lines of force and increases the strength of the field. A magnetic field can attract certain objects through solid wood and some other materials. It can exert force through a perfect vacuum. Every magnet or electromagnet produces a magnetic field.

### *Induction*

We have the whole science of electronics because a magnet produces a magnetic field. Yet we cannot really explain magnetism very well. We can only say how magnetism works, not why it works. One property of a magnetic field is of outstanding importance. If a small piece of wire is moved across the lines of force of a magnetic field, a small electric current flows in the wire. The kinetic energy of the moving wire is changed into electrical energy. The wire does not have to touch the magnet. All it must do is cut *across* the lines of force. The faster the wire moves the more electrical current runs in the wire. The more lines of force the wire cuts, the more electric current runs in the wire. This principle is called *induction.* An electric current is *induced* in the moving wire. Actually, the magnetic field is able to change mechanical energy into elctrical energy. Every electric motor, every electric generator, and every transformer depends upon this principle of induction.

REMEMBER

- A moving wire cutting the lines of force in a magnetic field produces an electric current in the wire.
- The more lines of force the wire cuts, the more current generated.
- The faster the wires move, the more electric current generated.

### **Electromagnetism**

If a wire is passed through a magnetic field, an electric current is produced. To reverse the process, if an electric current is run through a wire, a magnetic field is produced. This is called an electromagnet. You can test this principle by connecting the two terminals on a small battery with a bare wire. The wire will pick up iron filings while it is connected. If the wire is shaped into a loop, the shape of the magnetic field changes. Figure100 (A) shows the effect of the loop. Th lines of force are increased inside the loop. If more loops are added, the magnetic field grows stronger. A coiled wire carrying electricity that has more than one loop is usually called a *solenoid, or coil.* The coil will act like any other magnet. One end of the coil is positive; the other end is negative. Because the coil has two poles, we say that it shows *polarity.*

A solenoid acts just like a bar magnet. The strength of the magnet depends upon the size of the wire, the number of turns of wire, and the amount of electrical current running through the wire. An increase in any of these factors makes the magnet stronger. If an iron bar is placed inside the coiled wire, it concentrates the lines of force and makes the magnet much stronger. Most electromagnets have an Iron core.

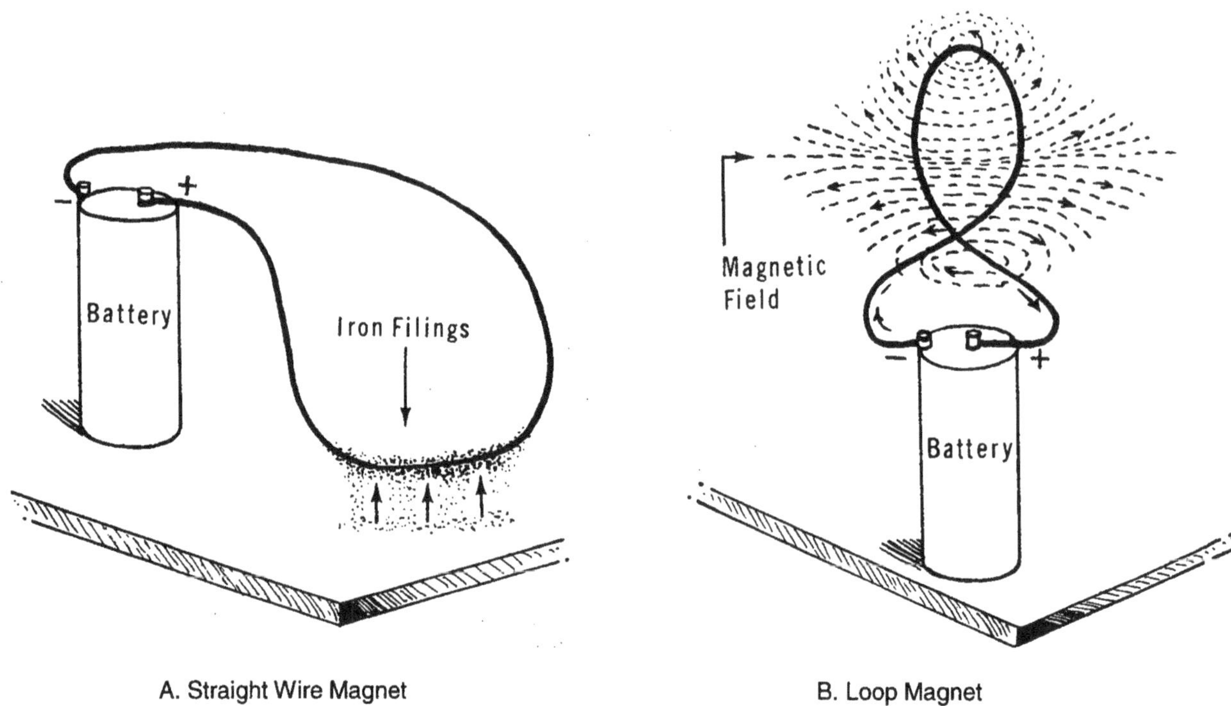


A. Straight Wire Magnet

B. Loop Magnet

FIGURE 2

### *Making Electricity*

When electrons flow through wire, an electric current is present. That is what we mean by electricity. Before electrons will flow, there must be an excess of electrons in one place, separated from an excess of protons. This makes a potential difference between the two points. To make electricity we must create a potential difference between two points. We can do this with a magnet and a length of WIre.

Let us place a large U-shaped magnet in a vice. Then we take a piece of copper wire and attach the wire to a sensitive meter that measures electric current. Now we move the wire down between the poles of the magnet. We have cut the lines of force, and we have created a potential difference inside the wire. For electrons will move from one end of the wire to the other. An electric current flows in the wire. If we move the wire back up between the poles of the magnet, the electrons flow back in the other direction. The magnetic field holds the electrons in position. When the wire moves, the electrons are strained apart. This produces the potential difference that causes electrical current to flow. And this is the way we change the mechanical energy of the moving wire into electrical energy.

### *The Alternating Current Generator*

Now let us put this principle to work. In figure 101, a simple electric generator is shown. There is a large magnet, with a loop of wire that rotates between the poles of the magnet. We must have some source of energy to spin the wire loop. The energy that spins the loop is converted into electrical energy by the generator. The generator is called an *alternating current generator.* The electrons flow first in one direction along the wire and then in the reverse direction.

Each complete turn of the wire loop is called one *cycle.* As the loop turns, the amount of electric current flowing in the wire varies in a regular pattern. If we follow the wire loop through one complete turn, or cycle, we can see how this change takes place.

In position A the wire loop is horizontal. It is not cutting any lines of force in the magnetic field. Therefore no electric current is flowing in the wire. As the loop turns from A to B, it begins to cut lines of force. More and more electric current flows in the wiare. When the loop reaches position

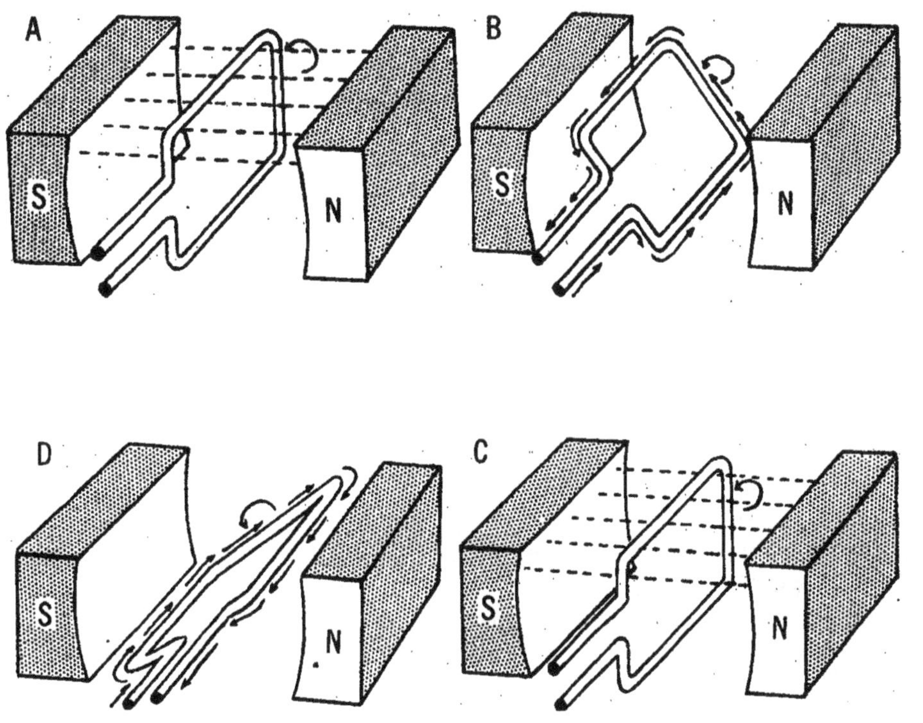


FIGURE 3. Loop Generator-Four Positions.

B, it is cutting all of the lines of force, and the current in the wire reaches a peak. Moving from B to C, the amount of current in the wire drops away to zero. The number of lines of force cut by the wire drops away to zero. When the wire is in position C, no current is flowing in the wire

The wire loop continues to turn from position C to position D. But this time the wires are reversed, and the current is flowing in the opposite direction. The amount of current increases once again to a peak at position D, but the current is flowing in the opposite direction in the wire. From position D back to position A, the current drops off once again. Back at position A, the current in the wire is zero, and one full cycle is complete.

***Tile Current Cycle***

We can draw a graph to show the amount of current flowing in the wire loop at different parts of the cycle. This graph is shown in figure 102. The graph begins at position A in figure 101. Each quarter turn of the loop is marked. Notice that the current reaches a peak after one quarter turn, and then returns to zero. In the next quarter turn, it reaches a second peak--*in the opposite direction.* Then it returns again to zero. Alternating current always has peaks in both directions because the current flows in both directions in the wire loop. The graph in figure 102 is called a sine wave. It shows one full cycle of electric current, produced by an alternating current generator.

The number of cycles of current produced each second is called the *frequency* of the electricity. In the United States most generators produce sixty full cycles of current each second. This is written sixty cps. For radio broadcasting, much higher frequencies are used. The radio

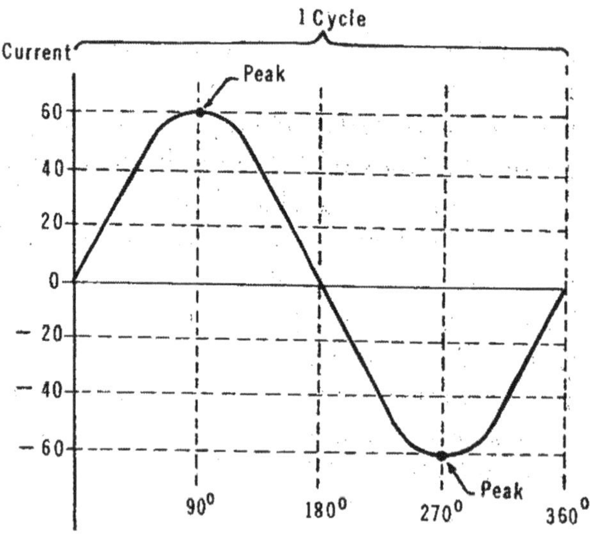


FIGURE 4. Graph: Sine Wave.

broadcasting band begins at 550 kilocycles, or 550,000 cycles per second. One kilocycle is equal to one thousand cycles. For special types of radio, a unit of one million cycles is used. This is called a *megacycle.* The human ear cannot hear these electrical frequencies. Our ears can be stimulated by mechanical energy only. Electrical energy has no effect on the ear.

### *The Electric Generator*

An electric motor and electric generator are nearly the same. The electric generator converts mechanical energy into electrical energy. An electric motor converts electrical energy into mechanical energy. Actually, electricity is not very useful until it is changed into another form. But it is easy to transport and store, and cheap to produce. This makes it an ideal form of energy for many purposes.

The magnetic field in an electric generator is supplied by an electromagnet called the field coil. This coil lies just inside the housing of the generator. The moving part of the generator (the loop) is called the *armature.* The armature is wound with many loops of wire. Some wire is always cutting the lines of force of the magnetic field and producing electric current. The ends of the loop of wire wound on the armature are attached to two *slip rings.* The electric current generated in the generator is taken off the armature from these two rings. They are in contact with two *brushes* which carry the current away from the rings. When the generator is used to produce *direct current,* which flows in only one direction, a device is used to reverse the connections after each half turn of the armature. This device is called a *commutator.*

The generator cannot produce energy. It can only convert mechanical energy into electrical energy. Some outside power must turn the armature. In large electric plants a steam turbine is used to turn the armature in a very heavy generator. In an automobile, the small generator is attached to the drive shaft of the car.

### *The Electric Motor*

The electric generator changes mechanical energy into electrical energy. The electric motor changes electrical energy into mechanical energy. The parts in a motor and a generator are nearly the same. But an electric motor depends on a different principle. A pole that has a positive charge is attracted to a pole with a negative charge. But it is repelled by another positive pole. This is the principle that runs an electric motor.

In an electric motor, electricity is fed into the field coil and into the winding of the armature. This creates two electromagnets, each with a positive pole and a negative pole. When the electricity is connected, the positive pole of the armature moves toward the negative pole of the field coil. This turns the armature. But the turning would stop as soon as the positive armature pole reached the negative field coil pole. So, when the positive pole has nearly reached its goal, the commutator on the motor reverses the current.

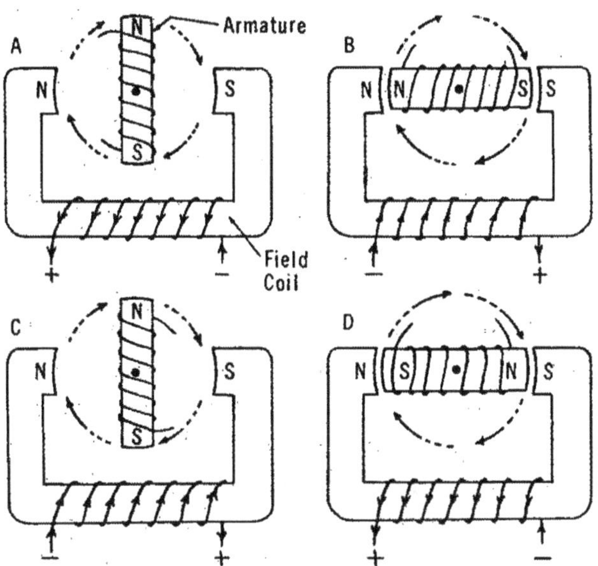


FIGURE 5. Electric Motor Showing Rotation

The positive pole on the armature is now facing a positive pole and is pushed away toward the negative pole. Again, just as it reaches its goal, the commutator reverses the connections. Again the armature pole is shoved away. So the armature keeps turning, trying to bring a positive and negative pole together. Because of the commutator it never succeeds. The pole on the armature is like a dog chasing a mechanical rabbit at a race track. Just as the dog reaches the rabbit, the rabbit's speed is increased and the dog falls bechind. The turning armature of the motor produces mechanical energy which can be used to do work.

***Transformers***

The electric line that passes your house carries about eighteen thousand volts. But inside the house it is a safe 110 volts. This voltage is produced by a transformer. A transformer also uses the principle of induction. But it uses it to move electricity from one wire to another even though the two wires are not touching. Inside a transformer there are two solenoids or coils. They are often wound around the same center.

One solenoid is connected to a source of alternating current. As the current moves through the coil, it produces an electric field around the coil. The electric field passes through the second coil nearby. As the current moving through the coil rises and falls with each cycle, the magnetic field

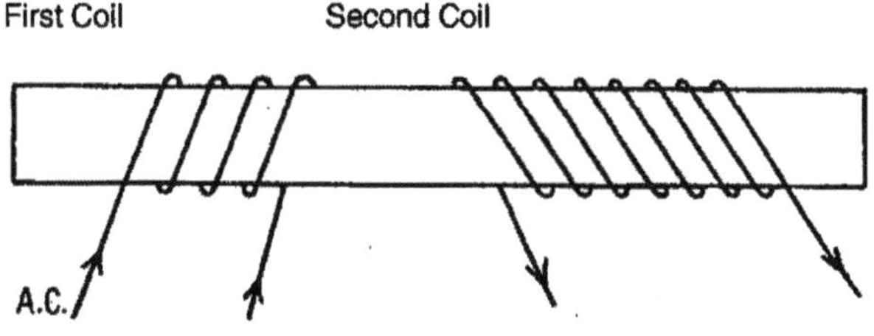


FIGURE 6. Principle of the Transformer.

around the coil also rises and falls. This produces an electric current in the second coil which is an exact duplicate of the electric current in the first coil. Although neither of the coils moves, the lines of force move as the field expands and collapses. As the lines of force cut across the wire in the second coil, they induce an electric current in the second coil.

The voltage in the second coil depends upon the number of turns of wire used in each coil. If there is the same number of turns in each coil, the voltage will not change as it moves from one to the other. If the second coil has ten times as many turns as the first coil, the voltage will be increased ten times. This is called a *step-up* transformer. If the number of turns in the second coil is 1/10 as large as the number in the first coil, only 1/10 as much voltage will be produced in the second coil. This is called a *step-down* transformer. Transformers can be used any time the voltage must be changed in an electric circuit. They are manufactured in a wide variety of sizes for different types of voltage changes.

### Words Used in Unit 2

**armature** (ăr´məchər), the moving part of a generator
**arranged** (ərănjd´), put into proper order
**collapses** (kə lăps´əz), shrinks together
**commutator** (kŏm´ū tă tər), device which reverses the direction of flow of electricity
**concentrates** (kŏn´sən trăts) , brings together to one place
**induced** (in dūst´), produced, caused to appear
**organized** (ŏr´gən ĭzd), put into working order
**repel** (rĭ pĕl´), force back, move away from
**terminals** (tər´mə nəlz), the ends of a battery where an electrical connection is made

# Batteries

## Unit 3

Science is full of surprises. We learned in the last unit that a spinning loop of wire in a magnetic field can produce electricity. It does this by separating electrons and protons to produce an electrical potential in the spinning wire. No liquids are used. No chemical reaction takes place. Yet electricity is produced. This seems to be a long way from the chemist's laboratory. Yet the chemist only smiles to himself. He fills a glass with a few chemicals dissolved in water. He places a rod of carbon and a rod of zinc in the water and attaches a wire to each rod. When the two wires are connected, an electric current flows through the wires. The chemist too can produce electricity.

There is a useful lesson in this for anyone who studies science. The chemist and the physicist start from different points. But they both deal with electricity, even though they use different approaches. You see nature is not divided into only chemistry and physics. Our environment is all one. We have divided our world into physical and chemical things. But electricity is only the flow of electrons along a wire. It does not matter how you cause the electrons to flow. The physicist does it one way; the chemist does it another. Both men produce electricity.

### *The Voltaic Cell*

When you start your car, you must use a battery to turn the engine over until the small electrical generator gets going. This battery produces electricity by a chemical reaction. We know that electricity is produced when there is a potential difference between two points. This occurs when electrons and protons, or positive and negative charges, are separated. The chemist separates his charges in a unit called the *voltaic cell*. All batteries are a variation of this basic unit.

The voltaic cell consists of three parts:

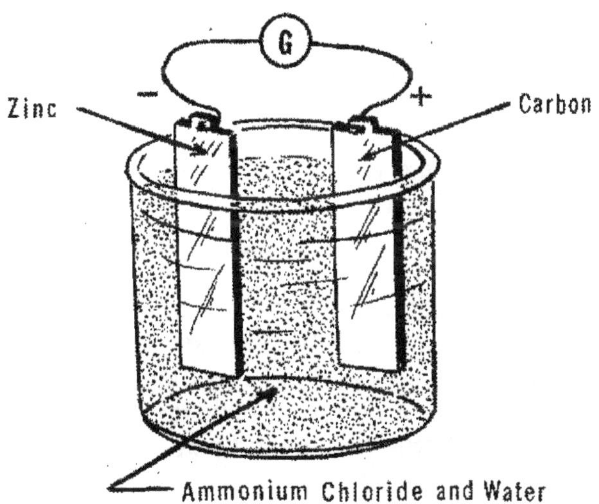


FIGURE 7. Voltaic cell

(1) a container made of insulating material-some material that will not conduct electricity; (2) a chemical solution called an electrolyte; and (3) two metal plates, called electrodes, which are placed in the solution. The electrodes must be conductors of electricity. When the electrodes are joined by a wire, electrons will flow along the wire. The voltaic cell will produce an electric current.

What happens inside the cell to produce electricity? One of the electrodes is made of the metal zinc. The other is made of pure carbon. The electrolyte is usually a mixture of water and sulfuric acid. Water is not a good electrical conductorthe sulfuric acid makes the solution a conducting material.

### *Chemical Action in Cell*

When the electrodes are placed in the electrolyte, the zinc plate dissolves. It forms charged particles called irns. Ions can be either positively charged or negatively charged. If there is a surplus of eleetrons on the ion, it is negatively charged. If there is a shortage of electrons on the ion, it is positively charged. You can probably see the connection already. Electricity is produced by a flow of surplus electrons. Anyhow, the zinc forms ions with a surplus of electrons. These surplns electrons gather on the zinc electrode. This gives the zinc electrode a negative charge.

The electrons taken from zinc are added to the zinc strip. So the zinc electrode acquires a surplus of electrons. There is still one more step. The water in the electrolyte produces hydrogen ions, or negative charges. These hydrogen ions move to the carbon rod and collect electrons from it. So the carbon rod gets a surplus of protons, or positive charges.

By chemical action we thus produce a positive charge on the carbon rod and a negative charge on the zinc rod. The zinc rod has an excess of electrons. And so there is a potential difference between the carbon rod and the zinc rod. If we conned these two points, electrons will flow from the zinc rod to the carbon rod. An electric current will be produced in the wire. As the electrons move from the zinc plate, more zinc dissolves and the potential difference is maintained. Eleetric current will flow from zinc to carbon until the zinc has completely dissolved. Then the voltaic cell will be worn out. A new zinc rod must be added to make it work again.

This is the basic method which the chemist uses to produce electricity. He dissolves zinc and uses the energy to produce electricity. Many kinds of material can be used to make a voltaic cell. Usually electrodes are made of zinc and carbon because both minerals are cheap. The electrolyte is often a compound of ammonia and chlorine called *ammonium chloride.*

### *Primary Cells and Secondary Cells*

When the zinc in the voltaic cell is used up, the battery is dead. A cell of this sort is called a *primary cell.* The chemical action inside the battery moves only in one direction. When the cell is unable to produce more electricity, nothing can be done to make the battery useful again.

There is another type of battery, however, which can solve this problem. The chemical action inside this battery cell can be reversed. When the cell is producing electricity, a chemical reaction takes place.

When the cell runs down, the chemical action can be reversed. We say that the battery is *discharging* when it is producing electricity. When the process is reversed, the cell is being charged. This type of battery is called a *secondary cell.* We know many examples of both batteries. A flashlight battery is a primary cell. When it is used up, we throw it away. An automobile battery is a secondary cell. It can be recharged again and again before it must be thrown away.

### *The Primary Cell --- A Dry Cell Battery*

The most common primary cell is the small battery we use in a flashlight. Usually it is made in the shape of a small cylinder. The outer shell of the battery is a small can made of zinc. This is the negative electrode of the battery. The positive electrode is a solid carbon rod suspended in the can. The carbon rod is insulated from the zinc can-they do not touch. Inside the can there is a damp paste of ammonium chloride and water. The cell is not completely dry, but it can be turned upside down without spilling. The top of the can is sealed with some plastic insulating material. This separates the carbon rod from the zinc can and holds in the electrolyte.

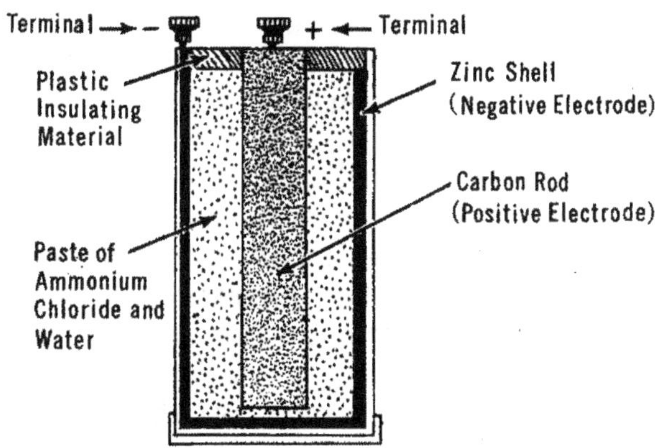


FIGURE 8. Dry Cell Battery

The dry cell works just like the voltaic cell. The zinc dissolves, and excess electrons form on the zinc can, and hydrogen ions take electrons from the carbon rod, creating a shortage of electrons on the rod. This produces a potential difference between the two points. When they are connected, electricity is produced in the connecting wire. When all of the zinc has dissolved, the cell is used up. These cells produce about one volt of electrical pressure and a small amount of electrical current.

### *Electrolysis*

The secondary battery cell is based on another principle. When an electric current is passed through a solution of water, the process is called *electrolysis.* The results of *electrolysis* depend on the dissolved materials in the solution. If the solution is a mixture of water and sulfuric acid, electrolysis produces hydrogen at one electrode and oxygen at the other electrode. In other words, electrolysis separates water into hydrogen and oxygen molecules. If the solution contains copper sulfate, electrolysis will produce pure copper on the negative electrode. The electric current separates the dissolved materials so they have an electrical charge. They then move toward the terminal of the opposite polarity, or opposite charge.

Because electrolysis will separate dissolved materials, it is often used to place a thin metal coating on a metal base. Silver plating and chromium plating are done by electrolysis. This is called *electroplating.* Let us look at one example of the process. When electricity is passed through a solution of copper sulfate, copper ions and sulfate ions are formed. The copper ions have a positive charge; the sulfate ions have a negative charge. The positive copper ions move to the negative plate, and the negative sulfate ions move to the positive plate. This movement takes place when electric current is flowing.

Direct current must always be used for electrolysis to keep the current moving in just one direction. If the negative plate in the tank is a piece of metal, a layer of pure copper will be deposited on the plate. Because the ions of copper are pure, this is a good method for separating copper from any impurities it may contain. So electrolysis is widely used in the copper industry to produce pure metal.

### *The Storage Battery*

The principle of electrolysis is used by the secondary cell to produce electricity. Electrolysis is made to produce a chemical change in a battery. When this chemical change is reversed, electricity is produced by the battery. Actually, the battery gives up the energy that caused the first chemical change. That is why it is often called a storage battery. It "stores" the electrical energy until its chemical process is reversed. Then it releases the energy.

How is this done? Let us take the automobile battery as an example. This is called a lead-acid battery because its main parts are lead and acid. This battery is an insulated case, containing an electrolyte and two plates. Both plates are made of the same material-lead. The electrolyte is a mixture of sulfuric acid and water.

Now, when the battery is made, both terminals are attached to lead plates. There is no potential difference between the two plates, and no electricity can be produced by the cell. Before the cell will produce electricity, it must go through electrolysis. A direct current is run through the battery. This causes a chemical change in one of the lead plates. It creates a potential difference between the two plates. This potential difference will produce electricity when the chemical reaction is reversed. Electrolysis is called *charging the battery.*

### *Grouping Battery Cells*

A single battery cell provides a small voltage and a little current. A commercial battery usually contains several separate cells, tied together into one unit. There are various ways to tie the batteries together. Each method gives different voltage and current ratings for the battery. If all the positive terminals and all the negative terminals are tied together, the connection is called a *parallel* connection. If the positive terminal of one cell is tied to the negative terminal of the next cell, the connection is called a *series* connection. If a combination of the two eonncctions is used, it is called a *series-parallel* connection. Each method has advantages and disadvantages. In general, a parallel circuit supplies high current rating, but no increase in voltage. A series circuit supplies high voltage and low current ratings. A series-parallel circuit can combine the advantages of both types of connection.

**Batteries**

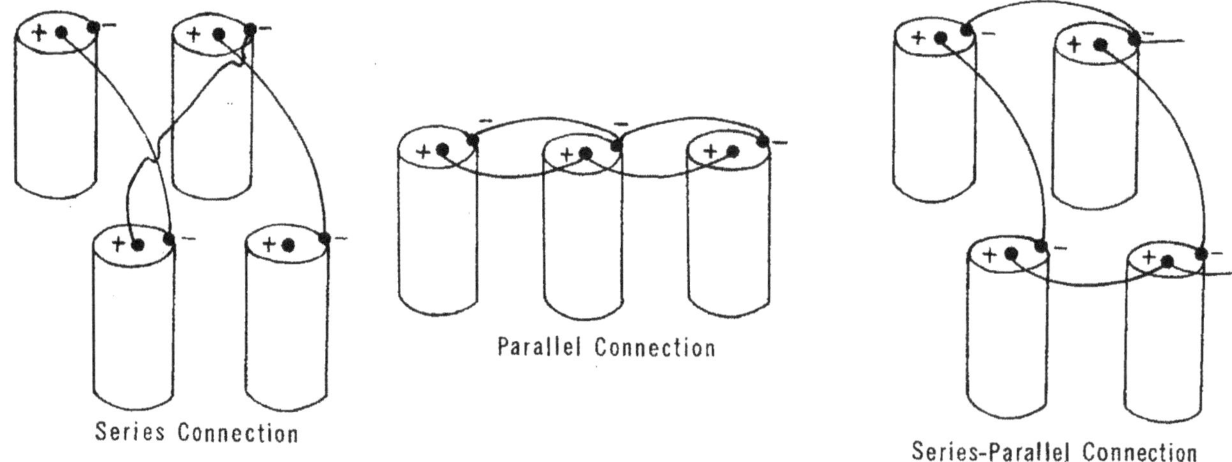


FIGURE 9. Series, Parallel, and Series-Parallel Connections.

### Words Used in Unit 3

**approaches** (əprōch´əz), ways of getting to something
**commercial** (kə məər´shăl), made to be sold
**electrolysis** (ĭ lĕktr´ŏlə sĭs), the passing of an electric current through a solution of water
**ions** (ī´ənz), electrically charged particles
**laboratory** (lăb´rə tŏ rĭ), place equipped for scientists to work
**surplus** (sər´pləs), amount over and above what is needed
**voltaic** (vŏl tā´ĭk), basic type of battery

# Using Electricity

## Unit 4

Electricity is energy. It can be used to do work. Electricity is probably the most convenient form of energy we have. It can be produced easily and cheaply. It can be transported from place to place rapidly and. economically. It can be changed into mechanical energy by a simple and inexpensive electric motor. Electric heat is clean and quickly produced. In many ways electricity is an ideal form of energy.

### *Producing Electricity*

Every year the United States uses about 600 billion kilowatt-hours of electricity. One kilowatt-hour is the amount of electricity needed to burn a thousand watt bulb for one full hour. Some of our electricity is produced by converting water power into electric power. Running or falling water is used to spin a large turbine. A generator converts this spinning energy into electrical energy.

Most of the electricity used in the United States is produced by burning coal. In the last few years, we have begun to use atomic power to produce electricity. Most atomic plants use the heat energy in a nuclear reactor to produce steam. The steam is used in a turbine, and the turbine spins a large generator. The generators used to make electricity commercially are very large and heavy. The armature may weigh thousands of pounds. The coils are made of thick heavy wire. A large generator can produce thousands of amperes of electric current under a pressure of ten thousand to fifteen thousand volts.

### *Transporting Electricity*

When electricity is transmitted for long distances, the voltage is always increased. The electricity is run through a step-up transformer. Then high voltage electricity is sent along heavy wires. This reduces the loss of energy in the transmission lines.

Electricity can also be transmitted without wires. But air has a very high resistance to electricity, and the losses are high. Wireless transmission of electric power is not yet practical. Radio waves are really electrical energy moving through air. But they must be produced at high frequencies. And the amount of energy that reaches a radio reeeiver is very small.

Long-distance electric power lines usually carry electricity at about 300,000 volts pressure. This high pressure cuts down losses. But it is too dangerous to use in the home. Three hundred thousand volts of pressure can force electricity through several inches of air, and cause an arc. This can be very dangerous. So the voltage is dropped for home use to 110 volts or 220 volts. Heavy appliances like stoves use 220 volt electricity because this reduces the relative amount of current flowing in the wires of the house. If a stove needs twenty amperes of 110 volt electricity, it needs only ten amperes of 220 volt electricity to produce the same energy. You can prove this by looking at Ohm's Law again. When the voltage is doubled, the current needed to produce the same power is cut in half. This makes for safer electrical operation.

### *Heating with Electricity*

Electricity is produced when electrons flow through a wire. The electrons are carrying energy, and they can do work as they flow. If we place a high resistance in the path of the electrons, they will work hard to get past it. This work generates heat. This is the basic principle behind all electrical heating systems. The higher the resistance, the more work the electrons must do to pass. This produces more heat. An English physicist named Joule studied the relation between resistance and heating power in electricity. He discovered three basic laws that seem to explain what happens when we heat by electricity. The three laws are:

- The amount of heat produced is directly proportional to resistance.
    - If one ohm of resistance in a cir- cuit produces one joule of heat, ten ohms of resistance will produce ten joules of heat. One joule is equal to 0.24 calories.

- The amount of heat produced is directly proportional to the time the current flows.
  - If one joule of heat is produced in one second, ten joules of heat will be produced in ten seconds.
- Heat produced in a circuit is directly proportional to the square of the current flowing in the circuit.
  - If two amperes of current produce four joules of heat, three amperes of current will produce nine joules of heat.

These three laws tell us that we can increase the amount of heat that is produced by an electrical circuit if we:

1. increase the resistance in the circuit.
2. increase the current in the circuit.
3. increase the time that current flows in the circuit.

Notice that an increase in current causes the greatest change in the amount of heat produced. That is why 220 volt electricity is used for heavy appliances. It reduces the current in the house wiring and reduces the amount of heat produced in the wires. This cuts down the danger of fire in the house.

***Lighting***

The electric light bulb was invented by an American, Thomas A. Edison. A light bulb is simply a piece of wire with a very high resistance and a high melting point which is placed inside an evacuated glass bulb. When electrons pass through the wire, they heat it white hot. The material must have a high resistance to produce the white heat. So it must have a high melting point too, or it will melt in the high temperature. Most light bulb filaments are made of tungsten wire. The filament is placed in a glass bulb, and most of the air is pumped out of the bulb. If the air remained in the bulb, the oxygen would burn the hot filament. Usually some inert gas like argon or nitrogen is placed in the bulb. This saves the filament and allows the use of higher temperatures.
Inert Gas

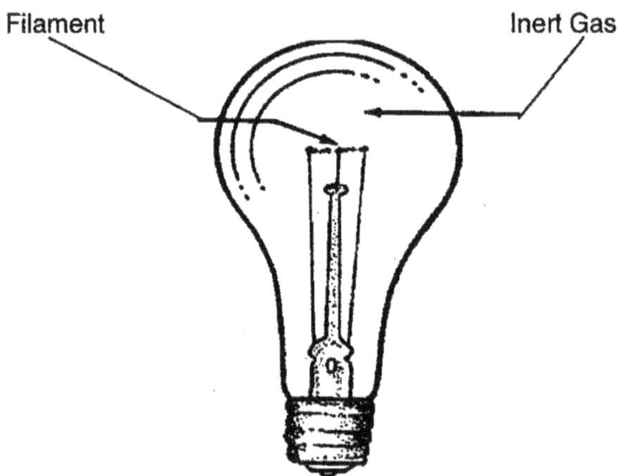


FIGURE 10. Light Bulb.

***The Telegraph***

Electricity travels at the speed of light --186,000 miles per second. This makes it an ideal carrier for messages. The first method of using electricity to carry messages was invented by Samuel F. B. Morse in 1837. Morse called his invention the *telegraph*. It uses the principle of an electromagnet. When an electric current flows through a coil of wire, the coil becomes a magnet, and it will attract metal. When the current is shut off, the magnet stops working. Morse used this simple principle to send his messages along electric wires.

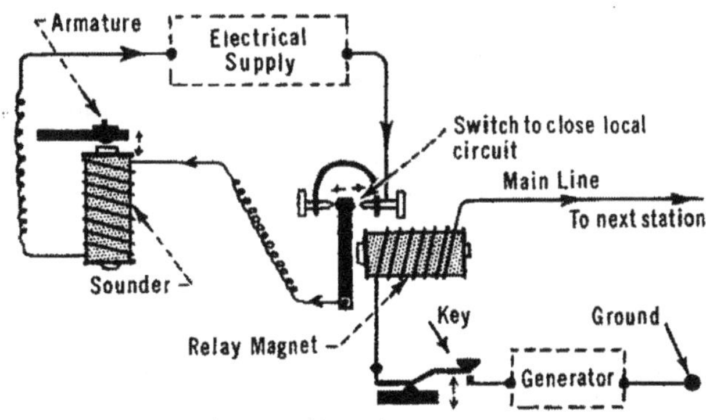


FIGURE 11. Simplified Telegraph with Key.

The main parts of a telegraph system are the key, the sounder, the wires, and a supply of electricity. These parts are shown in figure 109. When the key is pushed down, electricity flows through the wires and produces an electromagnet in the coil. This draws the sounder down with a sharp click. When the key is released, the magnet releases the sounder. By spacing the sounds made on the sounder, we can send messages. Morse also invented an alphabet made of long and short signals which is called the *Morse Code*. Using this code, we can send messages from one place to another. Of course, both the sender and the receiver must understand the Morse Oode-but it can be learned in a short time.

The old key and sounder system is not used much today. Instead, we use a machine that looks like a typewriter to send and receive messages. Each key of the machine sends a special signal along the wire. When that signal is received, the receiving machine types out the same message. These machines are called *teletype* machines. They are much faster and more accuurate than a key and sounder. They are used by the Armed Forces, police, news services, and many other organizations.

### The Telephone

The telephone is more complex than the telegraph. The telegraph works by changing the *amount* of energy sent over a wire. The telephone must do more than this. First, it must change mechanical energy, produced by the voice, into electrical energy. Then the electrical energy is transmitted over a wire. Finally, the telephone must change the electrical energy back to mechanical energy that our ears can hear.

The principle that a telephone uses to change mechanical energy into electrical energy is a simple one. According to Ohm's Law, when the resistance in a circuit changes, the amount of current flowing through the circuit changes. A telephone transmitter uses the mechanical energy in sound to change the electrical resistance in a circuit. The method is quite simple.

A round disc, or diaphragm, is attached to a small box filled with carbon particles. Carbon is a resistor, and it is part of the electrical circuit of the telephone. When the sound waves strike the disc, it vibrates. This compresses the particles of carbon. As the carbon particles are pressed together, the resistance in the circuit drops. When the pressure is released, the resistance in the circuit rises. This causes changes in the current flowing in the circuit. They follow the same pattern as the vibrations of the disc

The telephone receiver must change the electrical energy carried by the electric current into mechanical energy. We cannot hear electrical waves. Our ears respond only to mechanical waves in the air. The telephone receiver uses the principle of the electromagnet. The variations in electric current produced by the transmitter cause variations in the strength of the electromagnet in the receiver.

In a telephone receiver there is a small electromagnet. This magnet holds the thin disc in place. As the strength of the magnet varies, the disc vibrates. Since the strength of the magnet is varied by the electric current produced by the vibrating disc in the transmitter, the disc in the receiver vibrates in exactly the same way. These vibrations produce mechanical sound waves exactly like those that activated the transmitter. Electrical energy is changed into mechanical energy, and our ears hear the sound coming from the receiver.

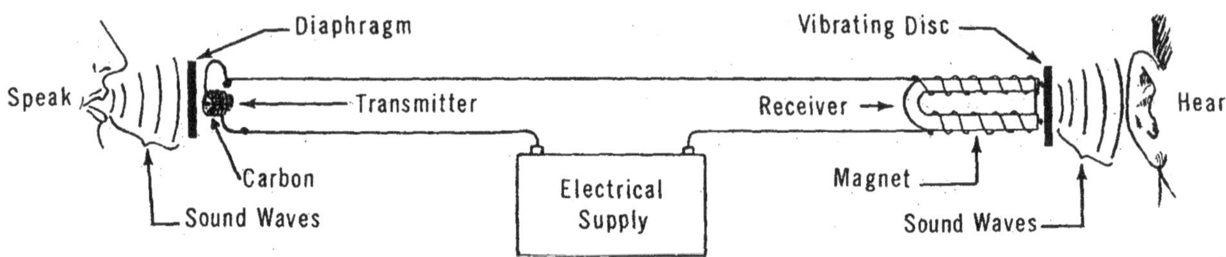


FIGURE 12 Simplified Telephone Circuit

## *Arc Welding*

There are so many possible uses of electricity that we can cover only a very few of them. In this unit we are looking at a few nonelectronic uses of electricity. One of the most important of these uses is arc welding. In modern industry arc welding is a very important process. It is employed to build auto bodies, airplanes, and thousands of other things that we use every day.

Electric welding works on the same principle as the electric arc light. High voltage and very heavy electric currents are needed for welding. Usually this requires a special transformer and a special electric line into the building. One end of the electric line is attached to the material to be welded. The other end is run through a special tip or rod made of high resistance metal. This rod is held by the man who does the welding.

There are different kinds of welding rods for each type of welding, depending upon the material to be welded. The composition of the tip or rod determines the strength of the joint and the temperature at the arc. A skilled welder chooses the rod that will best do the particular job. When the metal rod is touched against the material to be welded, the electric circuit is closed and electric current runs through the rod. The high resistance produces a high temperature, and the material in the rod is vaporized. This produces a trail of metal vapor between the rod and the material being welded. The heavy electric current runs through this vapor arc, producing a white heat.

As in the carbon arc light, the metal tip keeps melting as electricity flows along the rod. The vaporized metal forms a solid deposit on the joint, called a "bead." The tip of the rod must be kept an even distance from the material to produce a smooth, even joint. This takes experience and a steady hand. When the metal hardens and cools, it produces a joint that is very strong. In fact, the welded part of a joint is often stronger than the metal that is joined together.

## Other Uses of Electricity

Some of the special uses of electricity are often overlooked. It can be used to reduce smoke in cities, for example. If an electric device is placed inside a large chimney, it can be used to charge dirt particles as they move up the chimney. A collector higher up the chimney that has an opposite charge will collect the particles as they pass by. The amount of smoke and dirt that leaves the chimney is, thus, cut to a minimum. The collector must be emptied from time to time.

Electricity is very useful in the field of medicine. Special light bulbs are used to kill germs in hospitals. These lights produce energy of a particular frequency that is deadly to germs. Electric energy is used to provide heating for therapy machines, used to ease the pain when bones or muscles are seriously injured. There is even an electric knife that seals as it cut, thus eliminating the need for sewing. It is an excellent instrument for certain kinds of operations.

Radar and television, calculating machines, and weather satellites all come under the area of *electronics.* Yet all of these complex machines are built upon the same principles that are stated in Ohm's Law. The study of electronics is based on our study of electricity. The one great difference between electricity and electronics lies in making use of the effect that can be produced by a vacuum tube. But all electricity, whether it is passed through a vacuum tube or not, must obey the same general law.

**Words Used in Unit 4**

**economically** (ē kə nŏm´ĭk lĭ), inexpensively
**evacuated** (ĭ văk´ū āt əd), emptied
**filament** (fil´ə mənt) , the wire in a light bulb
**inert** (ĭn ərt´) , not active
**reduces** (rĭ dūs´əs), makes less
**transformer** (trăns form´ər), an apparatus for increasing or decreasing voltage
**vaporized** (vā´pər īzd) , changed into vapor, or a gas
**welded** (wĕld´əd), joined together by pressing while soft and hot

---

# CONTENTS



continued .........

## CONTENTS

# I. TROUBLESHOOTING DATA FOR GENERATORS AND MOTORS

## Section I. DC GENERATORS

### 1. Failure to Build up Voltage

| *Probable cause* | *Remedy* |
|---|---|
| Voltmeter not operating | Check output voltage with separate voltmeter. Replace voltmeter. |
| Open field resistor | Repair or replace resistor. |
| Open field circuit | Check coils for open and loose connections. Replace the defective coil or coils. Tighten or solder loose connections. |
| Absence of residual magnetism in a self-excited generator. | Flash the field. |
| Dirty commutator | Clean or dress commutator. |
| High mica | Undercut mica. |
| Brushes not making proper contact | Free, if binding in holders. Replace and reseat if worn. |
| Newly seated brushes not contacting sufficient area on the commutator. | Run in by reducing load and use a brush-seating stone. |
| Armature shorted internally, or to ground | Remove, test, and repair or replace. |
| Grounded or shorted field coil | Test, and repair or replace. |
| Shorted filtering capacitor | Replace. |
| Open filter choke | Replace. |
| Open ammeter shunt | Replace ammeter and shunt. |
| Broken brush shunts or pigtails | Replace brushes. |

### 2. Output Voltage too Low

| *Probable cause* | *Remedy* |
|---|---|
| Prime mover speed too low | Check speed with tachometer. Adjust governor on prime mover. |
| Brushes not seated properly | Run in with partial load, use brush-seating stone. |
| Commutator is dirty or film is too heavy | Clean, or if film is too heavy, replace brushes with a complete set of proper grade. |
| Field resistor not properly adjusted | Adjust field strength. Tighten all connections. Make shim adjustment. |
| Reversed field coil or armature connection | Check and connect properly. |

### 3. Output Voltage Too High

| *Probable cause* | *Remedy* |
|---|---|
| Prime mover speed too high | Check speed with tachometer. Adjust governor on prime mover. |
| Faulty voltage regulator | Adjust or replace. |

### 4. Armature Overheats

| *Probable cause* | *Remedy* |
|---|---|
| Overloaded | Check meter readings against nameplate ratings. Reduce load. |
| Excessive brush pressure | Adjust pressure or replace tension springs. |
| Couplings not alined | Aline units properly |

| Probable cause | Remedy |
|---|---|
| End bells improperly positioned | Assemble correctly |
| Bent shaft | Straighten or replace |
| Armature coil shorted | Repair or replace armature |
| Armature rubbing or striking poles | Check for bent shaft, loose or worn bearings. Straighten and realine shaft. Replace bearings, tighten pole pieces, or replace armature. |
| Clogged air passages (poor ventilation) | Clean equipment |
| Repeated changes in load of great magnitude. (Improper design for the application). | Generator should be used with a steady load application. |
| Unequal brush tension | Equalize brush tension |
| Broken shunts or pigtails | Replace brushes |
| Open in field rheostat | Repair or replace rheostat |

## 5. Field Coils Overheat

| Probable cause | Remedy |
|---|---|
| Shorted or grounded coils | Repair or replace |
| Clogged air passages (poor ventilation) | Clean equipment. Remove obstructions. |
| Overload (compound generator) | Check meter reading against nameplate rating. Reduce load. |

## 6. Sparking at Brushes

| Probable cause | Remedy |
|---|---|
| Overload | Check meter readings against nameplate ratings. Reduce load. |
| Brushes off neutral plane | Adjust brush rigging. |
| Dirty brushes and commutator | Clean brushes and commutator. |
| High mica | Undercut mica. |
| Rough or eccentric commutator | Resurface commutator. |
| Open circuit in the armature | Repair or replace armature. |
| Grounded, open- or short-circuited field winding | Repair or replace defective coil or coils. |
| Insufficient brush pressure | Adjust or replace tension springs. |
| Brushes sticking in the holders | Clean holders. Sand brushes. |

# Section II. DC MOTORS

## 7. Failure to Start

| Probable cause | Remedy |
|---|---|
| Open circuit in the control | Check for open. Replace open resistor or fuse. |
| Low supply voltage | Check with voltmeter and apply proper voltage. |
| Frozen bearing | Replace bearing and recondition shaft. |
| Overload | Reduce load or use larger motor. |
| Excessive friction | Check for air gap, bent shaft, loose or worn bearings, misalined end bells. Straighten shaft, replace bearings, tighten pole pieces, aline end bells. |

## 8. Stops After Running a Short Time

| Probable cause | Remedy |
|---|---|
| Failure of supply voltage | Apply proper voltage, replace fuses, or reset overload relay. |
| Overload | Check meter readings against nameplate ratings. Reduce load. |
| Ambient temperature too high | Ventilate space to reduce ambient temperature. |
| Overload relays set too low for application | Adjust relays for the application. |

## 9. Attempts to Start, But Overload Relays Trip Out

| Probable cause | Remedy |
|---|---|
| Motor field weak or non-existent | Check field circuit. Repair or replace defective field coils. Tighten all connections. |
| Overload | Check meter readings against nameplate ratings. Replace motor with one suitable to the application. |
| Relays adjusted too low for the application | Adjust relays for the application. |

## 10. Runs too Slow

| *Probable cause* | *Remedy* |
|---|---|
| Line voltage low | Apply proper voltage. |
| Bushes ahead of neutral plane | Adjust brush rigging. |
| Overload | Check meter reading against nameplate readings. Reduce load. |

## 11. Runs too Fast under Load

| *Probable cause* | *Remedy* |
|---|---|
| Weak field | Check field circuit. Replace open coils or open starter resistors. |
| Line voltage too high | Reduce line voltage. |
| Brushes off adjustment with neutral plane | Adjust brush rigging. |

## 12. Sparking at Brushes

| *Probable cause* | *Remedy* |
|---|---|
| Same as dc generator (par. 6) | Same as dc generator (par. 6). |

## 13. Overheating

| *Probable cause* | *Remedy* |
|---|---|
| Same as dc generator (par. 4 and 5) | Same as dc generator (par. 4 and 5). |

# Section III. AC GENERATORS

## 14. Noisy Operation

| *Probable cause* | *Remedy* |
|---|---|
| Unbalanced load | Balance load. |
| Coupling loose or misalined | Reline coupling and tighten. |
| Improper air gap | Check for bent shaft, loose or worn bearings. Straighten and realine shaft. Replace bearings. |
| Loose laminations | Tighten bolts. Dip in varnish and bake. |

## 15. Overheating

| *Probable cause* | *Remedy* |
|---|---|
| Overloaded | Check meter readings against nameplate ratings. Reduce load. |
| Unbalanced load | Balance load. |
| Open load-line fuse | Replace fuse. |
| Restricted ventilation | Clean, and remove obstructions to ventilation. |
| Rotor winding short-circuited, open-circuited, or grounded. | Check, and replace defective coil or coils. |
| Stator winding short-circuited, open-circuited, or grounded. | Check, and replace defective coil or coils. |
| Bearings | Check for worn, loose, dry, or overlubricated bearings. Replace worn or loose bearings, lubricate dry bearings, relieve overlubrication. |

## 16. No Output Voltage

| *Probable cause* | *Remedy* |
|---|---|
| Stator coils open- or short-circuited | Check, and replace defective coil or coils. |
| Rotor coils open- or short-circuited | Check, and replace defective coil or coils. |
| Shorted sliprings | Disconnect field coils and check ring-insulation resistance with megger. Repair. |
| Internal moisture | Check with megger and dry windings. |
| No dc voltage at the slipring brushes. (No dc exciter voltage.) | Check for defective switch or blown fuse in exciter feeder lines. Repair switch or replace fuses. Check feeder cables for opens or shorts. Repair connections or replace cables. Refer to FAILURE TO BUILD UP VOLTAGE (par. 1). |
| Voltmeter defective | Check with a voltmeter known to be working properly. Replace. |
| Ammeter shunt open | Replace ammeter and shunt. |

## 17. Output Voltage Unsteady

| *Probable cause* | *Remedy* |
|---|---|
| Poor commutation at sliprings | Clean sliprings and brushes. Reseat brushes. |
| Loose terminal connections | Clean and tighten all connections and contacts. |
| Maladjusted voltage regulator and speed governor | Readjust speed governor and voltage regulator. |

## 18. Output Voltage too High

| *Probable cause* | *Remedy* |
|---|---|
| Overspeeding | Adjust speed-governing device. |
| Overexcited | Adjust voltage regulator. |
| Delta-connected stator open on one leg | Remake connection, repair or replace defective coil or coils. |

## 19. Frequency Incorrect or Fluctuating

| *Probable cause* | *Remedy* |
|---|---|
| Speed incorrect or fluctuating | Adjust speed-governing device. |
| Dc excitation fluctuating | Adjust belt tension of exciter generator. |

## 20. Voltage Hunting

| *Probable cause* | *Remedy* |
|---|---|
| External field resistance in total out position | Readjust resistance. |
| Voltage regulator contacts dirty | Clean and reset contact points. |

## 21. Stator Overheats in Spots

| *Probable cause* | *Remedy* |
|---|---|
| Short-circuited phase winding | Check and replace defective coils. |
| Rotor off center. (Improper air gap.) | Check for bent shaft, loose or worn bearings. Straighten and realine shaft. Replace bearings. |
| Unbalanced winding circuits | Balance winding circuits. |
| Loose winding connections | Tighten winding connections. |
| Wrong phase polarity connections | Correct connections for proper phase polarity. |

## 22. Field Overheating

| *Probable cause* | *Remedy* |
|---|---|
| Shorted field coil or coils | Check and replace defective coil or coils. |
| Dc excitation current too high | Reduce exciter current by adjusting dc voltage regulator. |
| Clogged air passages (poor ventilation) | Clean equipment. Remove obstructions. |

## 23. Alternator Produces Shock when Touched

| *Probable cause* | *Remedy* |
|---|---|
| Reversed stator field coil | Check polarity. Make correction to connections. |
| Static charges or grounded stator field coil | Check generator frame-ground connection or connections, clean and tighten. Repair or replace stator field coil. |

# Section IV. AC INDUCTION MOTORS

## 24. Failure to Start

| *Probable cause* | *Remedy* |
|---|---|
| Circuit breaker or fuse open | Check for grounds. Close breaker or replace fuse. |
| Overload relay open | Wait until motor cools and relay closes. |
| Low supply voltage | Apply correct voltage. |
| Stator or rotor windings open or shorted | Check and replace shorted coil or coils. |
| Winding grounded | Check and replace grounded coil or coils. |
| Overload | Check meter readings against nameplate ratings. Reduce or install larger motor. |

## 25. Noisy Operation

| *Probable cause* | *Remedy* |
|---|---|
| Unbalanced load or coupling misalinement | Balance load and check alinement. |
| Air gap not uniform | Center rotor by replacing bearing. |
| Lamination loose | Tighten bolts. Dip in varnish and bake (chapter 4, par. 70). Repeat several times. |
| Coupling loose | Tighten. |

### 26. Overheating

| *Probable cause* | *Remedy* |
|---|---|
| Overloaded | Check meter readings against nameplate ratings. Reduce load. |
| Electrical unbalance | Balance supply voltage. |
| Open fuse | Replace line fuse. |
| Restricted ventilation | Clean. Remove obstructions. |
| Rotor winding shorted, open, or grounded | Check and replace defective coil or coils. |
| Stator winding shorted, open, or grounded | Check and replace defective coil or coils. |
| Bearings | Check for worn, loose, dry, or overlubricated bearings. Replace worn or loose bearings, lubricate dry bearings, relieve overlubrication. |

## Section V. AC WOUND ROTOR MOTORS

### 27. Runs Slow with External Resistance Cutout

| *Probable cause* | *Remedy* |
|---|---|
| Cables to control box have insufficient current-carrying capacity. | Replace with larger cables. |
| Open circuits in rotor, cables, or controls | Clean, remake connections, and repair. |
| Excessive brush sparking | Clean sliprings and reseat brushes. |

## Section VI. AC SYNCHRONOUS MOTORS

### 28. Failure to Start

| *Probable cause* | *Remedy* |
|---|---|
| Open fuse | Replace fuse. |
| Faulty starter | Check and repair or replace faulty contacts or contactor coils. |
| Low supply voltage | Apply correct voltage. |
| Bearings | Check for bent shaft or worn, loose, dry, or overlubricated bearings. Replace and realine bent shaft. Replace worn and loose bearings, lubricate dry bearings, relieve overlubrication. |
| Overloaded | Check meter readings against nameplate ratings. Reduce load or install larger motor. |
| Stator coil open or shorted | Repair or replace coil or coils. |
| Field exciter current is being applied | Make sure that field contactors are open, and that field-discharge resistors are connected. |

### 29. Runs Slow

| *Probable cause* | *Remedy* |
|---|---|
| Overloaded | Check meter readings against nameplate. Reduce load or install larger motor. |
| Low supply voltage | Apply correct voltage. |
| Field excited too soon | Adjust time-delay relay so that exciter current will not be applied until rotor reaches synchronous speed. |

### 30. Failure to Pull into Step

| *Probable cause* | *Remedy* |
|---|---|
| No field excitation. Open rotor coils. Exciter inoperative. Faulty field contactor. | Tighten or solder open or loose connections. Repair or replace defective rotor coils. Be sure field contactor is operating properly. |
| Overloaded | Check meter readings against nameplate ratings. Reduce load or install larger motor. |

### 31. No Field Excitation

| *Probable cause* | *Remedy* |
|---|---|
| Grounded or open rotor coil | Repair or replace rotor coil or coils. |
| Grounded or short sliprings | Check and reinsulate. |
| No output from exciter | See dc generator (par. 1). |

## 32. Pulls out of Step, or Trips Breakers

| *Probable cause* | *Remedy* |
|---|---|
| Low exciter voltage | Readjust voltage regulator on exciter to increase voltage. |
| Intermittently open or shorted cables | Check, and replace defective cables. |
| Reversed field coil | Check polarity. Change coil leads. |
| Low supply voltage | Increase voltage if possible. Raise excitation voltage. |

## 33. Hunting

| *Probable cause* | *Remedy* |
|---|---|
| Fluctuating load | Increase or decrease size of flywheel on load or loads. Increase or decrease excitation current. |
| Uneven commutator | Recondition commutator. |

## 34. Stator Overheats in Spots

| *Probable cause* | *Remedy* |
|---|---|
| Open phase coil | Check and repair or replace faulty coil or coils. |
| Rotor not centered | Check for bent shaft, loose or worn bearings. Straighten and realine shaft. Replace bearings. |
| Unbalanced circuits | Repair loose connections, or correct wrong internal connections. |
| Shorted coil | Check and replace faulty coil or coils. |

## 35. Field Overheats

| *Probable cause* | *Remedy* |
|---|---|
| Shorted field coil | Check and replace faulty coil or coils. |
| Excitation current too high | Reduce exciter current by adjusting dc voltage regulator. |

## 36. Overheating

| *Probable cause* | *Remedy* |
|---|---|
| Overloaded | Check meter readings against nameplate ratings. Reduce load or install larger motor. |
| Underexcited rotor | Adjust to rated excitation. |
| Improper ventilation | Remove obstructions and clean air ducts. |
| Improper supply voltage | Adjust to rated voltage. |
| Reverse field coil | Check polarity. Change coil leads. |

# Section VII. AC REPULSION-INDUCTION MOTORS

## 37. Failure to Start

| *Probable cause* | *Remedy* |
|---|---|
| Open fuse | Replace fuse. |
| Overloaded | Check meter readings against nameplate ratings. Reduce load or install larger motor. |
| Low supply voltage. Lead wires insufficient current capacity. | Apply correct voltage. Install larger lead wires. |
| Stator coil open | Check and replace open coil or coils. |
| Stator coil shorted | Check and replace shorted coil or coils. |
| Stator coil grounded | Check and replace defective coil or coils. |
| Centrifugal mechanism not operating properly | Disassemble, clean, inspect, adjust, repair or replace. |
| Incorrect brush setting | Locate neutral plane by shifting brushes until there is no rotation when current is applied. Shift brushes in the direction of the desired rotation, 1⅓ bars from neutral on 4-pole motors of ½ hp and smaller, and 1¾ bars on larger 4-pole motors. On 2-pole motors, set ⅓ bar farther than setting given above. |
| Bearings | Check for bent shaft or worn, loose, dry, or overlubricated bearing. Straighten and realine bent shaft. Replace worn and loose bearings, lubricate dry bearings, relieve overlubrication. |

## 38. Runs Slow

| *Probable cause* | *Remedy* |
|---|---|
| Overloaded | Check meter readings against nameplate rating. |
| Centrifugal mechanism not operating properly | Disassemble and clean. |
| Bearings binding | Clean and lubricate bearings. |

## 39. Overheating

| *Probable cause* | *Remedy* |
|---|---|
| Overloaded | Check meter readings against nameplate ratings. Reduce load or install larger motor. |
| Incorrect supply voltage | Apply correct voltage. |
| Centrifugal mechanism not operating properly | Disassemble, clean, inspect. Repair, adjust, or replace. |
| Bearings | Check for bent shaft, or worn, loose, dry, or overlubricated bearings. Straighten and realine bent shaft. Replace worn or loose bearings, lubricate dry bearings, relieve overlubrication. |

## 40. Noisy Operation

| *Probable cause* | *Remedy* |
|---|---|
| Bearings | Check for bent shaft, or worn, loose, dry, or overlubricated bearings. Straighten and realine bent shaft. Replace worn or loose bearings, lubricate dry bearings, relieve overlubrication. |
| Excessive end play | Adjust end-play takeup screw, or add thrust washers to shaft. |
| Motor not alined properly with driven machine | Realine. |
| Loose motor mounting and accessories | Tighten all loose components. |

## 41. Motor Produces Shock when Touched

| *Probable cause* | *Remedy* |
|---|---|
| Grounded stator coil | Replace defective coil or coils. Check motor-frame connection or connections to ground. Clean and tighten. |
| Static charge | Check motor-frame connection or connections to ground. Clean and tighten. |

# Section VIII. AC SPLIT-PHASE, CAPACITOR-START, AND TRANSFORMER-CAPACITOR MOTORS

## 42. Failure to Start

| *Probable cause* | *Remedy* |
|---|---|
| Open fuse | Replace fuse. |
| Low supply voltage | Apply correct voltage. |
| Stator coil open | Replace open coil or coils. |
| Centrifugal mechanism not operating properly | Disassemble, clean, inspect. Adjust, repair, or replace. |
| Defective capacitor | Replace capacitor. |
| Stator coil grounded | Check and replace grounded coil or coils. |
| Bearings | Check for bent shaft, or worn, loose, dry, or overlubricated bearings. Straighten and realine bent shaft. Replace worn or loose bearings, relieve overlubrication. |
| Overloaded | Check meter readings against nameplate ratings. Reduce load or install larger motor. |

## 43. Overheating

| *Probable cause* | *Remedy* |
|---|---|
| Shorted coil | Replace shorted coil or coils. |
| Centrifugal mechanism not operating properly | Disassemble, clean, inspect. Adjust, repair, or replace. |
| Incorrect voltage | Apply correct voltage. |
| Overloaded | Check meter readings against nameplate ratings. Reduce load or install larger motor. |
| Bearings | Check for bent shaft, or worn, loose, dry, or overlubricated bearings. Straighten and realine bent shaft, replace worn or loose bearings, lubricate dry bearings, relieve overlubrication. |

## 44. Noisy Operation

| *Probable cause* | *Remedy* |
| --- | --- |
| Worn bearings | Replace. Realine. |
| Shaft bent | Straighten shaft. Realine or replace rotor. |
| Excessive end play | Adjust screw of end-play takeup device, or put shim washers on shaft between end bells and rotor. |
| Loose motor mounts or accessories | Tighten all loose components. |

# II. TROUBLESHOOTING DATA FOR DC AND AC CONTROLLERS

## Section I. DC CONTROLLERS

### 45. Failure to Close

| *Probable cause* | *Remedy* |
|---|---|
| No power | Check power source. Replace faulty fuses. |
| Low voltage | Check power-supply voltage. Apply correct voltage. |
| Inadequate lead wires | Install lead wires of proper size. |
| Loose connections | Tighten all connections. |
| Open connections and broken wiring | Locate and repair or replace. Remove dirt from controller contacts. |
| Contacts affected by long idleness or high operating temperature. | Clean and adjust. |
| Contacts affected by chemical fumes or salty atmosphere. | Replace with oil-immersed contacts. |
| Inadequate contact pressure | Replace contacts and adjust spring tension. |
| Open circuit breaker | Check circuit wiring for possible fault. |
| Defective coil | Replace with new coil. |
| Overload-relay contact latched open | Operate hand- or electric-reset. |

### 46. Failure to Open

| *Probable cause* | *Remedy* |
|---|---|
| Interlock does not open circuit | Check control-circuit wiring for possible fault. Test and repair. |
| Holding circuit grounded | Test and repair or replace grounded parts. |
| Misalinement of parts; contacts apparently held together by residual magnetism. | Realine and test for free movement by hand. Magnetic sticking rarely occurs unless caused by excessive mechanical friction or misalinement of moving parts. |
| Contacts welded together | See paragraph 50, below. |

### 47. Sluggish Operation

| *Probable cause* | *Remedy* |
|---|---|
| Spring tension too strong | Adjust for proper spring tension. |
| Low voltage | Check power-supply voltage. Apply correct voltage. |
| Operating in wrong position | Remount in correct operating position. |
| Excessive friction | Realine and test for free movement by hand. Clean pivots. |
| Rusty parts due to long periods of idleness | Clean and renew rusty parts. |
| Sticky moving parts | Wipe off all accumulations of oil and dirt. Bearings do not need lubrication. |
| Misalinement of parts | Check for proper alinement. Realine to reduce friction, and test for free movement by hand. |

### 48. Erratic Operation (Unwanted openings and closures, and failure of overload protection)

| *Probable cause* | *Remedy* |
|---|---|
| Short circuits | Test and repair or replace defective parts. |
| Grounds | Test and repair or replace defective parts. |

| Probable cause | Remedy |
|---|---|
| Sneak currents | These are usually caused by intermittent grounds or short circuits in the machines or wiring circuit. Test and replace faulty parts or wiring. |
| Loose connections | Tighten all connections. Eliminate any vibrations or rapid temperature changes that may occur in close proximity to the controller. |

## 49. Overheating of Coils

| Probable cause | Remedy |
|---|---|
| Shorted coil | Replace coil. |
| High ambient temperature or poor ventilation | Relocate controller, use forced ventilation, or replace with suitable type controller. |
| High voltage | Check for shorted control resistor. Check power-supply voltage. Apply correct voltage. |
| High current | Check current rating of controller. Check for high voltage, above. If necessary, replace with suitable type controller. |
| Loose connections | Tighten all connections. Check for undue vibrations in vicinity. |
| Excessive collection of dirt and grime | Clean but do not reoil parts. If covers do not fit tightly, realine and adjust fasteners. |
| High humidity, extremely dirty atmosphere, excessive condensation, and rapid temperature changes. | Use oil-immersed controller or dusttight enclosures. |

## 50. Contacts Welded Together

| Probable cause | Remedy |
|---|---|
| Improper application | Check load conditions and replace with a suitable type controller. |
| Excessive temperature | Smooth off contact surface to remove concentrated hot spots. |
| Excessive binding of contact tip upon closing | Adjust spring pressure. |
| Contacts close without enough spring pressure | Replace worn contacts. Adjust or replace weak springs. Check armature overtravel. |
| Sluggish operation | See paragraph 47, above. |
| Rapid, momentary, touching of contacts without enough pressure. | Smooth contacts. Adjust weak springs. Where controller has "JOG" or "INCH" control button, operate this less rapidly. |

## 51. Overheating of Contacts

| Probable cause | Remedy |
|---|---|
| Inadequate spring pressure | Replace worn contacts. Adjust or replace weak springs. |
| Contacts overloaded | Check load data with controller rating. Replace with correct size contactor. |
| Dirty contacts | Clean and smooth contacts. |
| High humidity, extremely dirty atmosphere, excessive condensation, and rapid temperature changes. | See paragraph 49, above. |
| High ambient temperature or poor ventilation | See paragraph 49, above. |
| Chronic arcing | Adjust or replace arc chutes. If arcing persists, replace with a more suitable controller. |
| Rough contact surface | Clean and smooth contacts. Check alinement. |
| Continuous vibration when contacts are closed | Change or improve mounting of controller. |
| Oxidation of contacts | Keep clean, reduce excessive temperature, or use oil-immersed contacts. |

## 52. Excessive Arcing of Contacts

| Probable cause | Remedy |
|---|---|
| Arc not confined to proper path | Adjust or renew arc chutes. If arcing persists, replace with more suitable controller. |
| Inadequate spring pressure | Replace worn contacts. Adjust or replace weak springs. |
| Slow in opening | Remove excessive friction. Adjust spring tension. Renew weak springs. See paragraph 47, above. |
| Faulty blowout coil or connection | Check and replace coil. Tighten connection. |
| Excessive inductance in load circuit | Adjust load or replace with proper size controller. |
| Faulty capacitor | Replace with new capacitor. |

## 53. Pitting or Corroding of Contacts

| *Probable cause* | *Remedy* |
|---|---|
| Too little surface contact | Clean contacts and adjust springs. |
| Service too severe | Check load conditions and replace with correct size controller. |
| Corrosive atmosphere | Use airtight enclosure. In extreme cases, use oil-immersed contacts. |
| Continuous vibration when contacts are closed | Change, or improve, mounting of controller. |
| Oxidation of contacts | Keep clean, reduce excessive temperature, or use oil-immersed contacts. |

# Section II. AC CONTROLLERS

## 54. Failure to Close

| *Probable cause* | *Remedy* |
|---|---|
| No power | Check power source. Replace faulty fuses. |
| Low voltage | Check power-supply voltage. Apply correct voltage. Check for low power factor. |
| Inadequate lead wires | Install lead wires of proper size. |
| Loose connections | Tighten all connections. |
| Open connections and broken wiring | Locate opens and repair or replace wiring. Remove dirt from controller contacts. |
| Contacts affected by long idleness or high operating temperature. | Clean and adjust. |
| Contacts affected by chemical fumes or salty atmosphere. | Replace with oil-immersed contacts. |
| Inadequate contact pressure | Replace contacts and adjust spring tension. |
| Open circuit breaker | Check circuit wiring for possible fault. |
| Defective coil | Replace with new coil. |
| Overload-relay contact latched open | Operate hand- or electric-reset. |

## 55. Failure to Open

| *Probable cause* | *Remedy* |
|---|---|
| Interlock does not open circuit | Check control-circuit wiring for possible fault. Test and repair. |
| Holding circuit grounded | Test and repair or replace grounded parts. |
| Misalinement of parts; contacts apparently held together by residual magnetism. | Realine and test for free movement by hand. Magnetic sticking rarely occurs unless caused by excessive mechanical friction or misalinement of moving parts. Wipe off pole faces to remove accumulation of oil. |
| Contacts welded together | See paragraph 59, below. |

## 56. Sluggish Operation

| *Probable cause* | *Remedy* |
|---|---|
| Spring tension too strong | Adjust for proper spring tension. |
| Low voltage | Check power-supply voltage. Apply correct voltage. |
| Operating in wrong position | Remount in correct operating position. |
| Excessive friction | Realine and test for free movement by hand. Clean pivots. |
| Rusty parts due to long periods of idleness | Clean or renew rusty parts. |
| Sticky moving parts | Wipe off all accumulations of oil and dirt. Bearings do not need lubrication. |
| Misalinement of parts | Check for proper alinement. Realine to reduce friction and test for free movement by hand. |

## 57. Erratic Operation (Unwanted openings and closures and failure of overload protection)

| *Probable cause* | *Remedy* |
|---|---|
| Short circuits | Test and repair or replace defective parts. |
| Grounds | Test and repair or replace defective parts. |
| Sneak currents | These are usually caused by intermittent grounds or short circuits in the machines or wiring circuit. Test and replace faulty parts or wiring. |
| Loose connections | Tighten all connections. Eliminate any vibrations or rapid temperature changes that may occur in close ·roximity to the controller. |

## 58. Overheating of Coils

| *Probable cause* | *Remedy* |
|---|---|
| Shorted coil | Replace coil. |
| High ambient temperature or poor ventilation | Relocate controller, use forced ventilation, or replace with suitable type controller. |
| High voltage | Check for shorted control resistor. Check power-supply voltage. Apply correct voltage. |
| High current | Check current rating of controller. Make check for high voltage, above. If necessary, replace with suitable type controller. |
| Loose connections | Tighten all connections. Check for undue vibrations in vicinity. |
| Excessive collection of dirt and grime | Clean but do not reoil parts. If covers do not fit tightly, realine and adjust fasteners. |
| High humidity, extremely dirty atmosphere, excessive condensation, and rapid temperature changes. | Use oil-immersed controller or dusttight enclosures. |
| Operating on wrong frequency | Replace with coil of proper frequency rating. |
| DC instead of ac coil | Replace with ac coil. |
| Too frequent operation | Adjust to apply larger control. |
| Open armature gap | Adjust spring tension. Eliminate excessive friction or remove any blocking in gap. |

## 59. Contacts Welded Together

| *Probable cause* | *Remedy* |
|---|---|
| Improper application | Check load conditions and replace with a more suitable type controller. |
| Excessive temperature | Smooth off contact surface to remove concentrated hot spots. |
| Excessive binding of contact tip upon closing | Adjust spring pressure. |
| Contacts close without enough spring pressure | Replace worn contacts. Adjust or replace weak springs. Check armature overtravel. |
| Sluggish operation | See paragraph 56, above. |
| Rapid, momentary, touching of contacts without enough pressure. | Smooth contacts. Adjust weak springs. Where controller has "JOG" or "INCH" control button, operate this less rapidly. |

## 60. Overheating or Contacts

| *Probable cause* | *Remedy* |
|---|---|
| Inadequate spring pressure | Replace worn contacts. Adjust or replace weak springs. |
| Contacts overloaded | Check load data with controller rating. Replace with correct size contactor. |
| Dirty contacts | Clean and smooth contacts. |
| High humidity, extremely dirty atmosphere, excessive condensation, and rapid temperature changes. | See paragraph 58, above. |
| High ambient temperature or poor ventilation | See paragraph 58, above. |
| Chronic arcing | Adjust or replace arc chutes. If arcing persists, replace with a more suitable controller. |

| *Probable cause* | *Remedy* |
|---|---|
| Rough contact surfaces | Clean and smooth contacts. Check alinement. |
| Continuous vibration when contacts are closed | Change or improve mounting of controller. |
| Oxidation of contacts | Keep clean, reduce excessive temperature, or use oil-immersed contacts. |

## 61. Arcing at Contacts

| *Probable cause* | *Remedy* |
|---|---|
| Arc not confined to proper path | Adjust or renew arc chutes. If arcing persists, replace with more suitable controller. |
| Inadequate spring pressure | Replace worn contacts. Adjust or replace weak springs. |
| Slow in opening | Remove excessive friction. Adjust spring tension. Renew weak springs. See paragraph 56, above. |
| Faulty blowout coil or connection | Check and replace coil. Tighten connection. |
| Excessive inductance in load circuit | Adjust load or replace with more suitable controller. |

## 62. Pitting or Corroding of Contacts

| *Probable cause* | *Remedy* |
|---|---|
| Too little surface contact | Clean contacts and adjust springs. |
| Service too severe | Check load conditions and replace with more suitable controller. |
| Corrosive atmosphere | Use airtight enclosure. In extreme cases, use oil-immersed contacts. |
| Continuous vibration when contacts are closed | Change or improve mounting of controller. |
| Oxidation of contacts | Keep clean, reduce excessive temperature, or use oil-immersed contacts. |

## 63. Noisy Operation (Hum or Chatter)

| *Probable cause* | *Remedy* |
|---|---|
| Poor fit at pole face | Realine and adjust pole faces. |
| Broken or defective shading coil | Replace coil. |
| Loose coil | Check coil. If correct size, shim coil until tight. |
| Worn parts | Replace with new parts. |

## 64. Vibration After Repairs

| *Probable cause* | *Remedy* |
|---|---|
| Misalinement of parts | Realine parts and test for free movement by hand. |
| Loose mounting | Tighten mounting bolts. |
| Incorrect coil | Replace with proper coil. |
| Too much play in moving parts | Shim parts for proper tightness and clearance. |

# ANSWER SHEET

TEST NO. ______________ PART ______ TITLE OF POSITION ______________________________
(AS GIVEN IN EXAMINATION ANNOUNCEMENT - INCLUDE OPTION, IF ANY)

PLACE OF EXAMINATION ______________________________ (CITY OR TOWN) ______________ (STATE) DATE ______________

| RATING |
|---|
| |

USE THE SPECIAL PENCIL. MAKE GLOSSY BLACK MARKS.

| | A B C D E | | A B C D E | | A B C D E | | A B C D E | | A B C D E |
|---|---|---|---|---|---|---|---|---|---|
| 1 | A B C D E | 26 | A B C D E | 51 | A B C D E | 76 | A B C D E | 101 | A B C D E |
| 2 | A B C D E | 27 | A B C D E | 52 | A B C D E | 77 | A B C D E | 102 | A B C D E |
| 3 | A B C D E | 28 | A B C D E | 53 | A B C D E | 78 | A B C D E | 103 | A B C D E |
| 4 | A B C D E | 29 | A B C D E | 54 | A B C D E | 79 | A B C D E | 104 | A B C D E |
| 5 | A B C D E | 30 | A B C D E | 55 | A B C D E | 80 | A B C D E | 105 | A B C D E |
| 6 | A B C D E | 31 | A B C D E | 56 | A B C D E | 81 | A B C D E | 106 | A B C D E |
| 7 | A B C D E | 32 | A B C D E | 57 | A B C D E | 82 | A B C D E | 107 | A B C D E |
| 8 | A B C D E | 33 | A B C D E | 58 | A B C D E | 83 | A B C D E | 108 | A B C D E |
| 9 | A B C D E | 34 | A B C D E | 59 | A B C D E | 84 | A B C D E | 109 | A B C D E |
| 10 | A B C D E | 35 | A B C D E | 60 | A B C D E | 85 | A B C D E | 110 | A B C D E |

Make only ONE mark for each answer. Additional and stray marks may be counted as mistakes. In making corrections, erase errors COMPLETELY.

| | A B C D E | | A B C D E | | A B C D E | | A B C D E | | A B C D E |
|---|---|---|---|---|---|---|---|---|---|
| 11 | A B C D E | 36 | A B C D E | 61 | A B C D E | 86 | A B C D E | 111 | A B C D E |
| 12 | A B C D E | 37 | A B C D E | 62 | A B C D E | 87 | A B C D E | 112 | A B C D E |
| 13 | A B C D E | 38 | A B C D E | 63 | A B C D E | 88 | A B C D E | 113 | A B C D E |
| 14 | A B C D E | 39 | A B C D E | 64 | A B C D E | 89 | A B C D E | 114 | A B C D E |
| 15 | A B C D E | 40 | A B C D E | 65 | A B C D E | 90 | A B C D E | 115 | A B C D E |
| 16 | A B C D E | 41 | A B C D E | 66 | A B C D E | 91 | A B C D E | 116 | A B C D E |
| 17 | A B C D E | 42 | A B C D E | 67 | A B C D E | 92 | A B C D E | 117 | A B C D E |
| 18 | A B C D E | 43 | A B C D E | 68 | A B C D E | 93 | A B C D E | 118 | A B C D E |
| 19 | A B C D E | 44 | A B C D E | 69 | A B C D E | 94 | A B C D E | 119 | A B C D E |
| 20 | A B C D E | 45 | A B C D E | 70 | A B C D E | 95 | A B C D E | 120 | A B C D E |
| 21 | A B C D E | 46 | A B C D E | 71 | A B C D E | 96 | A B C D E | 121 | A B C D E |
| 22 | A B C D E | 47 | A B C D E | 72 | A B C D E | 97 | A B C D E | 122 | A B C D E |
| 23 | A B C D E | 48 | A B C D E | 73 | A B C D E | 98 | A B C D E | 123 | A B C D E |
| 24 | A B C D E | 49 | A B C D E | 74 | A B C D E | 99 | A B C D E | 124 | A B C D E |
| 25 | A B C D E | 50 | A B C D E | 75 | A B C D E | 100 | A B C D E | 125 | A B C D E |

Printed in the USA
CPSIA information can be obtained
at www.ICGtesting.com
LVHW072124261223
767470LV00008B/250